Today is a Good Day for Marshmallows

Today is a Good Day for Marshmallows

- a mother's memoir -

Kristi Hellenbrand

Printed in the United States of America

ISBN 978-1-257-71567-1

For Chelle, my sister…who first suggested to me
that writing a book would be within my reach.

For Brandon, who gifted me all of those mommy nights…
you inspired me to pause and listen, you pushed when I sat too long,
and ultimately you have given me my happy place.

For Tristan, Blake and Brooklynn…
without whom this book would not exist…
my precious babies, I do love you so.

Your children are not your children.
They are the sons and daughters of Life's longing for itself.
They come through you but not from you,
And though they are with you yet they belong not to you.

You may give them your love but not your thoughts,
For they have their own thoughts.
You may house their bodies but not their souls,
For their souls dwell in the house of tomorrow, which you cannot
  visit, not even in your dreams.
You may strive to be like them, but seek not to make them like you.
For life goes not backward nor tarries with yesterday.

-KAHLIL GIBRAN, The Prophet

contents

introduction

This all started as a journey into the heart of my family. It was a rather cool, rainy day in March 2008. I was sitting by myself in a cozy, aroma-saturated coffeehouse literally steeping in the midst of a self-examination of my life's rollercoaster ride through wifehood and parenthood. I was marveling at the ways in which my three lovely children can bring such joy and delight one moment and make me feel so puzzled and discouraged the very next. The day before had been one of those gorgeously simple days full of love, laughter, and an excitement to match that which early spring always brings. The chill of the morning had quickly dissipated leaving one of those delightfully warm early spring days that are reminiscent of why my husband and I moved to Georgia almost ten years ago - and never left. The kids and I had spent the morning painting at the kitchen table making our first masterpieces of spring. Then we spent the afternoon bird watching, squirrel chasing, and opening our sand box for the first time that calendar year. There was not a squabble to be heard or a boo-boo to kiss, just simply the bliss of a young mother enjoying the company of her children.

Then the sun set on that fairytale moment, however, and upon rising the next day brought pure madness and mayhem. Biting, screaming, crying and chaos had, sadly, defined this new day. So I sat by myself that evening ruminating over what had gone wrong. What had I done differently to allow for the past twenty-four hours to have gone so poorly? Why did those wonderfully beautiful, intelligent angels of mine morph into creatures from the swamp? And more importantly, why did *I* then become a swamp monster myself joining in on their tantrums as if I had time-warped back to being two years old? Would these strained moments between us define our family?

I believe that most parents have a genuine desire to hold steady through stressful times and ultimately be a beacon to their children. I have discovered however, that staying the course can be extremely difficult. Before being a mother I felt so powerful, so in control of my life. I cooked what I wanted to eat, I went where I wanted to go, the house was clean because I kept it clean, and certainly my emotions were within my own control. I purposefully kept company with those individuals that built me up and avoided at all cost those that threatened to pull me under. In short, I had created a steady and predictable life for myself. More than ten years later, having added a husband, three children, and two dogs to my life I have found that what I cook is yucky, where I go is boring, and clean has become a relative term. Keeping company with people that are not fighting, screaming, complaining or pouting is impossible unless I choose to follow the lead of that infamous mother who pulled her vehicle over and ordered her kids out. Trust me when I say that I have been in the same place, emotionally speaking. I have just chosen to kick them out of the vehicle while keeping the car in park.

There is no telling which strength of character I am required to draw upon at any given moment while raising these kids of mine. In fact, I often find my *weaker* talents or outright failings magnified to the "nth" degree instead. If I was an impatient person before children, I am an intolerant one now. If I was controlling before, I am damn right bitchy now. Everything is magnified a bit, a little rougher around the edges, we'll say. Stress can do that to people, of course, and children are stressful. They are worse than belligerent colleagues or angry friends, because they are *yours.* I find it ironic however, that to the same degree my children magnify my weaknesses, they also bring to light the brightest of my strengths. I find myself having the utmost of forgiveness available to them, I seem more agreeable to even the silliest things (I mean, I *did* watch the Wonder Pets cartoon a record six times with them this past rainy day) and I honestly and completely love them more than I've ever loved anything in my life.

What concerns me though, especially after a day like the one I described, is if I will be strong enough or steady enough when my kids need me the most. I worry if I will be the rock they can count on when the going gets tough, or if I will be waving the white flag of surrender with my face in the dirt. When they tease, bite or make growly faces at each other I frequently attempt to hurl words of wisdom their way, often find myself pleading for the Golden Rule, and occasionally just growl back at them if the two former have not worked. Honestly though, sometimes I find myself at a loss for a solution at all. That is when I begin to brood. I may outwardly let the offense go with a shrug of the shoulders, but inwardly there is a deep feeling of defeat. That night I finally asked myself the question: *Should I feel defeated though*? By allowing one of their sassy scowls or grumpy growls to go without comment, am I creating an unruly teenager? A disrespectful adult? A narcissistic citizen? I feel a tremendous weight on my shoulders for them to be and act perfect, as if every bit of bad attitude or lack of manners exhibited by my four-year-olds is due to one of my mistakes or missteps as their mother. I fed them too much sugar, I let them stay up too late, I allowed them to negotiate and I paid them for their household chores. Does this mean that my children will not turn into healthy, dependable, outstanding citizens in their lifetime?

All of those self-help books suggest we hold the power in our hands to make or break these little human beings. They keep telling me to stay the course and I will reap the benefits. After years of parenting with a particular goal in mind (The Perfect Child, of course), I wonder what it would feel like to go easier on them and myself. What if I sit back and observe and *honor* who these little ones are, and remember that they are *little ones* after all. Rather than being the navigator of all things in their lives, up to and including their moods, what if I allow them to discover for themselves *who they are*? What if I ride the waves instead of charting the course? Of course I will insist on some core family values: respect, honesty and the Golden Rule, but what about the rest of those unseen and often unreasonable expectations I have? I am fairly certain that I have growled at people before, even if it was just with my eyes. I can hardly fault them for expressing their frustrations, can I? One of my kids is very vocal, the other is more of a moper. I recognize that life is hard for these little guys with all the rules, expectations, and places to go and people to meet. We are all entitled to a bad day, aren't we?

Parents, universally I think, find themselves creating more drama in their households when we fight the innate people our children *are,* and try to make them something *we want.* Maybe we want them to be more outgoing, less shy around strangers or other children at the park. Maybe we wish they had more natural sports ability, or that they were more popular at school. Taller, stronger, brighter, more talkative, less talkative, bookish, less bookish, sweeter, or huggier, even. Maybe we want them to play the piano, chess, or sing like a songbird. Why else do we put them in Little League at age four, or in ballet class at three years old? Why do we expect them to read before Kindergarten and stand still at a ninety-minute church service when they are three years old? Most parents have an unspoken expectation of which personality traits and talents their children should have and the sad truth is that *most children do not live up to those ideals.* What if we let those expectations go? Ease up a bit. Honor them for who they are and have their back *even when they are wrong*. Let them have their bad days, let them lose their cool from time to time. Can we as a family come out of that journey stronger in self-identity and steadier in our own shoes, realizing that we are venerating their true self? Lead them by example, nurture them, sure. Love them, always. But what if we choose to focus on their strengths and forgive them their transgressions? Will the course be less rocky and quite possibly more *real* in the end?

My girlfriend Laura (another mother of twin boys and a little girl) commonly shares The Look with me, when our children have just been caught doing yet another obscenely irresponsible or foolish act. Her eyes roll up just a bit, her eyebrows meet her hairline and her shoulders shrug about an inch, clearly and quite accurately reflecting the "It is what it is" viewpoint she has of parenthood. We might have just had a particularly painful play date when the kids all fought with each other. Four boys sword fighting with only three swords never ends well and the girls are in tears over who gets to be the princess and who has to be the prince. The snack might not be right, or it might be late in coming. The loser of the game is a poor loser, or one of the boys might have just showed his bare booty to the rest of them and inspired a Bare Booty Race through the halls. "It is what it is" is a powerful explanation for all of the ups and downs inherent with raising children. It is empowering, even, suggesting we should go with the flow more, stop pretending we know best, help them up if they fall, guide them if they are lost, but ultimately follow their lead and honor their uniqueness. And most importantly for any left-brained moms out there, recognize that a synonym for irresponsible and foolish is *childish*.

As I am approaching my mid-thirties I find myself drawn to this type of living more and more. I think of the children's animated movie <u>Nemo</u>, when Marlin and Dory are frantically searching for their lost little clown fish and they find themselves going deeper and deeper into the ocean where soon there is only blackness around them. Marlin is freaked. He is yelling, waving his fins around with a helplessness and frustration that many mothers can easily relate to. In stark contrast Dory just keeps plugging along singing her song, "Just keep swimming, swimming, swimming…" There are days as a parent when my mountain of responsibilities or even my own unrealized endeavors and dreams, seem to pull me deeper into the darkness and despair of anxiety and sadness. Now tack on the very real possibility that at that very moment my children might decide to spontaneously start their own fight club, and it is easy to relate to Marlin at those moments. I have thrown my hands up in the air, sobbed, or screamed about how unfair it all is. The fact of the matter though is that I want to be Dory. Deep inside me I want the strength to pause, breathe and see it for what it is. Usually it is trivial and small, occasionally it can be far bigger, but the key is recognizing that my reaction can be to act like Marlin and stay lost in one place or I can choose to change course and reach the surface where there is light, and air and reprieve. Just keep swimming, girl!

In hindsight I realize now that I sat in that coffeehouse that night thinking about how to be a better *me*, forgetting that this journey is not all about me. I will no longer be so pretentious as to assume I have the lone power to make or break my children's destiny. Today's moodiness will not determine tomorrow's successes or failures. The good the bad and the ugly will all serve us in some way to becoming the people we (and our children) are meant to be. The family we are meant to be. True, I want to commit to memory the heavenly moments of these fleeting years when my children are young, but I also want to honor the complexity of this journey and ultimately enjoy discovering who my little ones will grow up to be.

The other discovery I made that evening at the coffeehouse was that I have a genuine desire to share these uncharted waters and the application of my hopes and dreams with other mothers. I found a deep wanting to record in written words the sugar and spice of our family life, while giving necessary respect to the snakes and snails and random animal tails that tend to rear their ugliness from time to time. I wondered if I might learn a few lessons while recording our life together, and even enjoy a few laughs. I have come to a place in my life where I firmly believe that our lives are deserving of a good long pause and a sigh of contentment. I want to honor our imperfections and simply live deliberately. I want to take a break from all of the self-help mothering books that are lined up on my bookshelves and instead turn my studying gaze on the people around me. Rather than looking at each day as a hospital triage, pigeonholing the day into urgent and important lists of necessary accomplishments, I want to stop and *literally* smell the flowers - or maybe the sweaty "boy dirt" that has permeated every cell on my son's shoulder on this warm spring day. The tangy, earthy smell of my daughter's hair, just after a bath, when she is curled up on my lap is just so delicious that I have decided to take special note of it today. When I pause a bit, when I decide to ride the waves of our life together like a surfboarder, honoring the pull and push of the comfortable shore while still being aware that there may be an unseen squall on the other side of the island, I rediscover the beauty of motherhood, and quite possibly life in general. Upon doing this I realized, actually *felt,* that our story was worth sharing.

I saw one small problem when it came down to it, however. I am not a writer. My uncle, an English teacher and at one time a sort of mentor of mine, probably has a coronary every Christmas when he receives my attempt at a holiday newsletter. Grammar is questionable, misspellings are assumed and content is always a little sketchy. So this would be quite an endeavor for me to write down *our lives.* I have never been one to journal. Having said that, I must admit that I did, in fact, have three diaries collecting dust that probably had, in total, about ten pages with written words on them. During the first thirty years of my life if I got the urge to pick up a diary it was because I needed to complain about something. Writing down your frustrations is supposed to be cathartic. The therapeutic result of those writings was successful, I think. The problem is that nobody, me included, wants to go back and read *that* journal entry. It is a depressing and usually lonely account of a victim in the throws of confusion. As a book-lover and a budding history-lover, the discovery of a journal in the dark recesses of a long forgotten drawer at first appears to be a rare gem, a treasure of sorts. However, upon reading one of these potential lost treasures full of past ramblings about an altercation with my spouse, mother or friend, I discover that rarely do I wish to rehash it. It's like watching a bad movie twice. So the day that I threw away those old journals was like the final exam for a college course entitled, Letting Bygones be Bygones 101. I still appreciate the process of writing down my problems and venting on paper, especially if it saves the people I love from hearing those grievances over their dinner plate each night to a chorus of dramatic moaning and synchronized eye rolling. What I do now however, with these gripes that I pen down is *throw them away* afterwards.

So this project of mine, a written scrapbook of sorts, was really new territory for me. To sit down and write what amounts to the blood, guts, heart, and soul of our family life, while not focusing on the toxic concoction of moaning and groaning I'm so familiar with, was a challenge I was ready to face. My story is not one of great grief, abuse, secrets, illness, loneliness, or political strife. I have been blessed to have skirted around most of these malicious misadventures in the course of my young life. I thank God every day that I have yet to experience most of those tragedies that fill our bookshelves and bestseller's lists. That's not to say that my life is boring and I promise that the recount of it will not be like watching <u>Groundhog Day</u> on the USA network.

My story is a life journey of a power-hungry, perfectionist mother learning to live her best life by giving up the reins. A journey of determining what is important in this life, and letting the rest go. I will not allow my errors, my missteps to define my family or me. Parenting these little ones of mine can sometimes feel akin to standing on the edge of the Grand Canyon, mesmerized by its simple beauty yet terrified of a misstep. It should not be so. The misstep need not be feared. Respected, maybe, but not feared. My husband, Brandon and I have also learned and accepted over the course of our ten years cohabitating, that marriage can be much the same. The intimacy of the relationship can intoxicate us like banana daiquiris enjoyed with the sting of sunshine on our shoulders, while the day-to-day grind of sharing space and idiosyncrasies threaten to pull us into the surf without the benefit of a red flag warning. Slowly, and with much hesitation, my husband and I are beginning to understand that those paradoxes are what define a life *lived* versus a life spent just surviving. We all enjoy the chill of winter more if we have also experienced the glow of summer, after all.

A tidbit of information you may find helpful to explain my perspective on things; spontaneity does not come easy for me. My particular genetic make-up prefers order, planning and rarely do I crave a surprise around the bend. Being a good mother requires me to relax that type-A personality a bit, loosen the strings that bind me, and welcome adventure even if it is not always asked for, planned on or even enjoyed. At the end of the day, these little adventures and even misadventures seem to be what weave our lives into a tapestry worth recounting and remembering. Most appreciated and often forgotten is that children can find adventure in even the most ordinary things: a picnic blanket on the first day of spring, frogs caught by a creek, even an electric screwdriver discovered in a previously un-ransacked kitchen drawer. The ordinary is *extra*ordinary to our children. The culmination of any given day's worth of work on this book continues to surprise me because there are a plethora of ordinary moments turned extraordinary that I have chosen to respect by slowing down and hushing up. Those moments could just as easily have been missed or simply forgotten if I was the same woman that sat in that coffeehouse just a few years ago.

What I did not want this book to be was yet another record of vacations, birthday parties or other supposedly momentous events in our family life. Our photo albums and video cameras already document those happenings to the extent that every photo album looks remarkably like the last, with the exception that my daughter's piggy tails are a little longer and Daddy's hair is a little thinner. What most of us fail to document in any meaningful way are the ordinary events of our day to day lives, even when *those* are the moments that truly define us as a family. Humor me for a moment. My propensity to rise each morning an hour before my children, coffee cup in my still sleep-warmed hands, reading Time Magazine with a look on my face that my husband says can only be described as "mole-ish" is what begins each morning within the walls of our home. The tilt of my daughter's head and the twinkle in her eyes each time she earnestly pleads her case for yet *another* snack is the hourly routine for the next ten waking hours of each day. The perfect lines of my oldest son's hamstrings as he is poised on the arm of the sofa for yet another launch (wearing only his Wall-E underwear) is the view from my desk on our family's average afternoon. *This* is what defines my ordinary yet extraordinary family.

Creating a tangible record of these memories is empowering as a mother. I was *paying attention*. I was honoring the simple joys and challenges of motherhood at the moments I penciled these down. Whether these are memories that my children will appreciate having written down, I cannot pretend to know. I do know that some of my own memories from childhood are not those that I would have logically expected to remember. My father enjoys hearing my recollections, as they are different from his own. Cinnamon rolls and hot chocolate each Sunday after church at O'Malley's Farm Café made church an event worth surviving each week. Peeking in at him while he did headstands with yoga music playing and his weight loss chart hanging on the wall, always put me in awe of his physical strength and stamina. Watching my mother tend her garden, smiles of delight over each green bean or raspberry found. These particular memories make me wonder why my brain chose *them* to engrave on my gray matter where other events slipped through some filter never to be heard from again. When I hear my father's smile over the phone as I relay these memories it is priceless. All of my birthday parties run amuck in my brain, but I can clearly recall the afternoon my sister and I arranged every pillow my family owned on the floor of our house and carried on as "rock" hopping fools for hour upon hour. Next we were werewolves chasing each other and then we were frogs on lily pads. We laughed and enjoyed each other tremendously that afternoon. I want my own children to know that I took notice of their similarly mundane but fantastical days and hope that one day they may read my account of each of their distinctive charms, amusing feats, and pleasurable moments, and smile.

My hope however, for you the reader, is that maybe, just maybe, my life story will help you with *your* life story. When I reveal my weaker moments as a mother, I hope you may be comforted to know that I too, am an Imperfect Mother. Every day I come closer to respecting my weaknesses and honoring them, instead of feeling run over by them. Quite possibly, my mistakes will inspire you to do better than I have, or maybe to forgive yourself of your most recent infraction. Maybe you will be less judgmental of yourself, but also less critical of your sister, neighbor or struggling friend who is also a mother doing this job with no required how-to manual. In addition, I share within these pages moments when I *must have done something right.* Against all odds (according to those how-to parent books), these little children I am raising are turning out to be lovers, artists, scientists, and comics. I sincerely hope you get a good laugh while reading some of the expressions, perspectives, and antics that every new day brings in my home. Twin boys by nature can bring a smile to most faces (and a cringe to others). I admit to cringing myself when I found my boys flooding my van's muffler with the hose up the tailpipe. I will save *that* story for later. There are other more profound life lessons that have brought me to my knees, squeezing each and every tear from my body, leaving me spent and empty inside. My life has been far from perfect and I have made my fair share of mistakes and both received and delivered heartbreak. I will share a few of these experiences with you as well.

My son Blake, in many ways, inspired this project. He is a reflective soul himself and has proven himself far wiser than what the average lifespan of four years usually allows for. When he was only three years old he began to exonerate himself from trouble by suggesting I remember all of the deliciously adorable things about him. *"But remember Mama...I'm a really good jumper* (hence why a launch from a kitchen table is appropriate)...*and I grew taller when I was sleeping last night* (hence why swimming in the deep end is okay*) ...and remember Mama I do give the best hugs!"* (Even if I just bit my brother.) All of this was said with a twinkle in his eye and a three-year-old equivalent of a wink, of course. When my patience had run out later that day and my own fiery temper resulted in behavior that in all fairness should have put *me* in time-out, I did not receive *his* version of a thundercloud in return. Instead I heard him say, with more grace than I had mustered all day, *"It's okay, Mama. Remember, I love you all the time."* If ever there was a reason to slow down and pause, the extent of this wisdom and grace delivered by my usually goofy and ever active three-year-old is it. Most of us, in the midst of the daily grind, rarely hear from our child that they love *us* unconditionally, even if we clearly are unworthy of a Best Mother Award.

Perusing the shelves of my local bookstore, I was surprised to find few memoirs like mine: stories about real women living with their average, everyday family doing their average, everyday stuff. Yes, I am in all likelihood, average. Yet I *feel* extraordinary. The dreams, the headaches, the love, the frustrations, the spontaneity and the routines of my every day are something to be proud of. Regardless of whether we are working full-time and lucky to get dinner on the table, or we are home all day with our munchkins yearning for alone time, we are doing extraordinary work. So, for all of you young mothers out there, I dedicate this book to you. We all have a story to tell. This is just my story.

One word of warning, if I may. There are many books for mothers on "how to." How to raise a healthy child, how to raise a "green" child, how to raise a strong-willed child, and the list goes on and on. This is *not* that kind of book. In fact, this book has plenty of, "do *not* try this at home" stories. The moments we wish we could take back, the words we wish we could have swallowed instead of spit out in anger, I recount a few of those. I have shared with you the real wishes of a real mother on any given *real* day. For example, I would have paid a lot of money to have a solo cup of coffee this morning without a raucous game of dinosaur checkers to referee. It just was not meant to be. So rather than feeling railroaded or suffocated by the depths of the selflessness motherhood requires, I choose to just keep swimming like little Dory. As a mother and wife I have come to expect the rollercoaster ride, even though I still feel both exhilarated and nauseous afterwards. Our bumpy breakfast was easily trumped by something my oldest son said to me when I picked him up from school. Tristan had picked a flower for me off the playground earlier that morning, and was madly digging through his backpack to present it to me. His eyes filled with tears when he found it dead and wilted at the bottom of his bag. *"It's not beautiful anymore, Mama."* My heart grew an inch wider, my hand gently cupped his tear- streaked cheek and I whispered, *"You* are beautiful."

That is the stuff that can give us the courage to tackle tomorrow and the day after that. At that very moment, for each of us, there should be a mandatory pause where the world's axis tilts a little in our favor, and we can smile knowing we are doing a good job. So I invite you to come on this crazy ride with me full of ups and downs, twists and turns, even the unexpected shoe-falling-off kind of stuff. At the heart of it will be the simple, extraordinary life of a young mother trying to do her best by her husband and children.

chapter one

what's the percent error in that?

I was living six hundred miles north of Atlanta and a twelve-hour drive away from my husband when I found out I was pregnant with my first child in February of 2003. Motherhood was something I had been dreaming about and planning for since before Brandon and I were even married and sharing the same residence. I was one of those child magnets at family gatherings, being reprimanded right along with my nieces and nephews for being too rowdy or loud and generally disturbing the peace of the adults around us. I had worked alongside children for many years doing various babysitting gigs and even working for a childcare establishment during a summer of college. I knew what little ones needed, what they craved and what I could deliver. In short, I thought I had it all figured out.

Alas, no. I was far from having it all figured out. In autumn of 2002, while still nursing a strong desire to have a child and begin our family, I was rudely relocated to a suburb of St. Louis in order to complete my doctorate of chiropractic. Graduation was supposed to be only three months away, in the spring of 2003, from Atlanta's LIFE University. Instead, I was looking at an extra nine months of classes and internships due to accreditation issues that were primarily of a political nature and completely unfounded, I might add. Eighty percent of the student population at LIFE U. was scrambling to other universities to finish their training, many leaving spouses and loved ones behind to man the mortgage and preserve the lives we all hoped to return to after graduation.

It was, for obvious reasons, a very difficult decision to leave my happily married husband back in Georgia and move to St. Louis for what could be an entire calendar year in a very young marriage. However, having spent four years of undergraduate school living and breathing a long distance relationship (and coming out the other side of it still intact) we had the fortitude to grab the bull by the horns and forge forward. We signed a short-term lease for a two-bedroom apartment which I would share with two of my fellow students, Nancy and Mike. Many a weekend had been spent in their company, drinking beer over a campfire, enjoying one of Nancy's healthy concoctions of beans and rice, and generally taking pleasure in each others' company. This arrangement allowed Brandon to rest easy because I would not be alone in a strange city. We even agreed that I would keep one of our dogs with me at the apartment to preserve the flavor and feel of home.

What we did not speak about during the process of establishing my new residency was the elephant in the room: that *baby* we had been trying to make for almost two years. At first we just figured we were not getting the timing right. Increased frequency of baby-making effort was Brandon's suggestion, met with a roll of the eyes and a grin from his wife. In the end, there was no one thing, physiology, tighty-whities, or otherwise, that explained why, at the young age of twenty-five, I was unable to conceive a baby. Inordinate amounts of stress always topped the lists we were given by our doctors as a predictor for difficulty in this department, so when the accreditation issues began and my expensive doctorate degree was up in the air it was an unspoken given that there would be no baby coming in our near future.

Two weeks after purchasing a second bed and making the long and exhausting move to Missouri, I was taking a shower after a long day of classes when I discovered how tender and sore to the touch my breasts were. Thinking I needed a new sports bra, I went to bed that night feeling inordinately tired and homesick. It was at least a week later when my fatigue really kicked in that I started to put the pieces of the puzzle together. I had lost my appetite but had been assuming it was due to the same stress visible on *all* of the LIFE transplant's faces. Not so. Three weeks after committing to a one year hiatus in Missouri, I sat in wonder and awe (and complete frustration) holding a pregnancy test with that little blue line I had been praying for for two years. The move away from my husband was my first lesson in how unpredictable life can be. That little positive pee stick was my second lesson.

A carpool ride home with other LIFE-ers the following weekend found Brandon and me sitting at our kitchen table together, happy to be back under the same roof if even for just two days. In my absence he had started to take up his woodworking hobby again and had asked me to print an example of a bookshelf that I would like for our expanding office space. I instead presented him with a printout of a baby crib.

It took us a few weeks to weigh the pros and cons of completing my education while nine months pregnant and with a newborn occupying space in my rental, versus coming home to have my baby in the same geographic state as my husband resided, doctorate be damned. Really we were just in too much shock to make *any* decision more complicated than what was for dinner. I did, however, move home to Georgia in February of 2003, to the applause of my family and friends, vowing that if I had to walk dogs in my spare time we would make this financially risky and yet necessary first step in family preservation. Coming home was indeed, a breath of fresh air. We decided that school could wait but this baby-making business could not. There were unknowns a mile long, some of which we had forethought to consider and others we were too naïve to have on radar at all. I was leaving behind a four-year doctorate degree to potentially walk dogs, waitress in the evenings and raise our baby. Survival instinct kicked in, I suppose, because I was too sick (spending every other morning curled up into a ball, forehead wet with perspiration) to even care about the long term consequences that may include loan forbearance. The nausea was unrelenting, the stress was supposed to be bad for the baby (which in turn stressed me out), and frankly I was probably having physical symptoms of withdrawal from the interruption in coffee consumption that I had voluntarily imposed on myself. Life was crazy, but at least Brandon and I were back living in the same zip code.

It was three weeks after returning home to Georgia when the state courts announced that the lawsuit involving LIFE University's accreditation was unfounded and therefore dropped. My senior year program was resuming as usual, in just a few short weeks! Not only would I walk the stage for my graduation in three months time, I would follow it up with holding my baby in my arms just a couple of months after that. Wow. It was all going to work out after all. The past *six months* of tears, fears and frustrations was coming to an end. I reflected on how much my life looked more and more like a television Life Time drama series than I was all together comfortable with. It was all very surreal. Why, I asked myself, had my life become so clearly blessed?

At this point I feel I need to acquaint you better with my dear husband, Brandon, the engineer. This man is as left brained as they come, loving the inherent problem solving that tends to greet the human race on a day-to-day basis. He likes efficiency, perfection, and how-to manuals. Yes, I said *manuals*. A new remote control for our satellite television requires a full hour of my husband's playtime to discover all of its hidden potential. In contrast, I would prefer a brief thirty seconds of instruction where only the top five functions are explained. Brandon likes to take things apart, improve them in some small way, and put them back together again. Until I married this guy I had no idea there were so many options for toilet flushing handles, or that they could be set to so many different flush levels. So when we discovered that I was actually growing a baby in that ever-expanding tummy of mine, I wrongly assumed that Brandon would be frantically paging through Sear's The Baby Book like a fish out of water, looking for all the best ways to build and deliver a healthy baby. Boy was I wrong. He read about five pages in the book his mother gave him entitled, Fatherhood, set it down and never picked it back up. I swear that the process of simply holding the book put him straight to sleep. The only baby book he actually read was the required reading for our Bradley birthing class. And he only agreed to participate in the class because his crazy wife had decided she wanted to have this baby of theirs *at home*.

Yes, I wanted a homebirth. Having spent four years of my life learning in chiropractic school about all the things that can go wrong in a hospital setting (both in birth and death, it seems) I still have a healthy respect for the place, but also a fear. If I am bleeding or missing a body part, I will gladly occupy a bed in an emergency room. Those brilliant doctors will stop the bleeding and/or replace the body part. Amen to that. What I do not agree with is going to the hospital with an *otherwise healthy* baby about to be born, where they may mess with the process that nature has so eloquently handled to perfection thus far. I knew the medically documented likelihood of a C-section if I opted for a drug-induced labor to keep my baby on some doctor's schedule. I knew that if I wished to have a painless labor, the drugs gifted to me would also prevent me from standing upright or even squatting, dangerously abolishing the wonderfully brilliant law of gravity that might otherwise help my baby along the birth canal. And even after our baby graced us with its presence, I wanted to spare it the unnecessary physical assaults that happen every day to our newborns in our hospitals. Knowing without a doubt that I did not currently suffer from Hepatitis B, nor would my newly born child be promiscuous in its first few years of life, the Hepatitis B vaccine was entirely unnecessary and in my opinion was an assault to its immune system. We would forgo the silver nitrate sting to our newborns eyes, preferring for him or her to actually *see* us in the first few hours of life for healthy mother-baby bonding. I did sign up for the PKU test, but discovered through research that the test is in fact more accurately measured at one week old rather than one hour old, so our pediatrician later in the week would handle that one.

Instead of blinding lights, bossy white coated coaches and antiseptic smells, I wished instead for a dimly lit room where my body would begin and end its laborious work surrounded by love and a sense of calm and wonder. I never fully read the infamous book, <u>What to Expect When You Are Expecting</u>, because in truth that book shows you what to be *fearful* of when you are expecting. All the things that can go wrong during birth are the running themes of most of the popular birthing books. As a healthy alternative, I wanted to surround myself with the knowledge of what so often can and does go right. So we found a wonderfully experienced and warm midwife, named Claudia, only an hour from our home and we began the round of customary prenatal visits to gauge the health and well-being of both mommy and baby. For those of you thinking that this is where you set down the book and never pick it back up because this woman is kooky…keep reading. I concede that many would find me eccentric in my birthing choices. I concede that I do not always follow the road most traveled. In this case however, I sadly found myself right back on the straight and narrow against my utmost wishes…bear with me while I finish the story.

My school attendance carried on as usual, along with my clinical work with patients. Although my waistline continued to expand and my breasts became as large as small cantaloupes, I felt as healthy as I have every felt in my life. I walked my dogs every afternoon, even taking some short bike rides with Nancy and Mike (who had also returned to Georgia for classes and whom we had opened our home to until graduation). We went hiking in north Georgia at Tallulah Falls, a good three mile hike to the top of the waterfall and back, leaving me fatigued and winded but otherwise in good health. My appointments with the midwife always showed average measurements for size, normal urine tests and often times our sessions together became more of a mentoring session between a well-seasoned mother and a soon-to-be new mother.

Over the course of the next few months Brandon and I found ourselves really enjoying the newness of this baby-making thing. A mixture of awe and excitement led to a nesting that took over our nights and weekends. We were painting the baby room, assembling the crib, stroller shopping, laundering everything baby related with

Dreft, and generally baby proofing our home. We quickly discovered that stroller selection was tantamount to buying your first car. Color, weight, storage capability, ease of folding, and of course Consumer Report ratings all went into our standard Graco selection. When we finally walked out of the store feeling satisfied our future child would ride in comfort and safety, my lovely husband read and reread the accompanying instruction manual and spent the rest of the afternoon assembling said baby transportation. It was a victorious day.

The beautiful spring weather in Georgia had already come and gone, the azalea blooms having fallen away to the earth in their yearly recycling. We were in the thick of summer, now mid-July, when the air is so thick with humidity that you are wet with sweat within minutes of stepping outside. Porch fans no longer suffice to keep the heat at bay, leaving air conditioning and/or a water hose as the only viable options for cooling oneself. This is the time of year in Georgia when flip flops melt on the hot asphalt, popsicles are a mainstay of the summer food pyramid, and swimsuits are required attire. I was nine weeks out from my due date when the obligatory baby shower was scheduled. Being that the vast majority of our family still lived in Wisconsin, it was decided that the shower should be held up there to encourage participation in the event. The thought of escaping to a temperate warm summer weekend in the Midwest surrounded by our family and friends happily sent us packing.

I had one final appointment with my midwife prior to our fifteen-hour drive north, simply to confirm I was safe for such sustained travel. Pee stick? Clear. Subjective complaints? None. Tummy measurements? Ummm…..Huge. Say what? Upon further poking and prodding, I was found to be *significantly* larger at 31 weeks gestation than is customary. Speculation ensued. The immediate thought was that my body was producing too much amniotic fluid, nothing to be overly excited about but something Claudia felt needed to be confirmed with an ultrasound prior to our nine hundred mile road trip. Have I mentioned that this would be my *first* ultrasound? Until this point I had been *observably* pregnant, there was no need for a medical camera to confirm the presence of a baby in my uterus. Brandon and I had made the decision that we would utilize ultrasound only if we felt it was medically necessary for diagnosis, believing there was no reason to expose the fetus to unnecessary heat or agitation. At 31 weeks, measuring far larger than was typical, we had what we considered a valid reason to take a closer look at our precious baby. I scheduled the ultrasound for the following day with my back-up medical OB/GYN. We will call him Doc Angel.

Brandon took the afternoon off work to accompany me to the appointment. We were going to get our first and *only* peek at our little one and of course we wanted to celebrate the moment together. Deciding beforehand that we did *not* want to know the sex of the baby, we were led into the ultrasound tech's room. With the warm jelly on my belly, the computer screen facing us (the expectant parents!), the excitement was palpable. Our ultrasound technician was very professional and yet very warm, almost humming a song while chit-chatting with us. Yes, she assured us, it was common to have extra fluid. Yes, she could measure the fluid to know if there was reason for concern. The image came up and then there was the expected pause in conversation, while she rolled the camera wand over my belly. "Hmmmm..." she stalled. Then she grinned There it was! The baby's head was down very low in my pelvis, just as Claudia had found him/her to be. There was the perfect little nose, eyes and a smooth forehead resting on...what was that? Our tech eloquently outlined the fine, delicate skull of our baby, labeling it Baby A. Then she pointedly outlined the skull upon which Baby A's was resting deep in my pelvis and labeled it Baby B. Twins!

For some reason I cannot pretend to understand, it came as no shock to me that there were two little people in there. My heart rate did not skyrocket and my palms did not sweat. Somewhere deep within myself I think I already knew. Claudia had mentioned in passing, the day before, that it was possible there were two babies when I measured so large, but there was only one discernable heartbeat (she checked many times and in many locations) and quite frankly there was only one palpable fetus. Two arms, two legs, a head and one hiney was all she was able to detect in my placid belly. She explained that another baby could be hiding deep within my pelvis, but she felt it highly unlikely since I had measured so exactly perfect up until now. I had laughed a bit with Brandon the night before when I explained that there was a miniscule chance that there were two in there, but given Claudia's level of expertise we went with the likely Extra Fluid Diagnosis.

My husband's response to the ultrasound's disclosure of twins was far different from my own. First, he almost fell off his seat. When his rump was back firmly on the stool, he leaned forward at the computer monitor and with all seriousness said, "Yeah, but what's the percent error of this?" God bless him, he is an engineer after all. She smiled, and to substantiate her claims showed us two beating hearts, just inches from each other. Nope. No chance of error, Honey. Statistically, we had a 100% chance of *two* little babies coming out of that tummy of mine. And statistically *sooner* than the previously memorized due date.

So began the whirlwind of parenthood that we call our lives. For Brandon, the physical act of disassembling the single baby stroller and replacing it with the doublewide version, confirmed for him the new road we were on together. The road where one baby becomes two, a home birth becomes a hospital birth with the honoring of a birth plan that only Doc Angel would have agreed to uphold. A road where all the baby books in the world could not have prepared us for our first up-all-night-parenting or the breastfeeding-two-4lb.-babies-in-class-to-walk-at-graduation experience that defined the last month of my professional schooling.

No, as much as we think we have it all under control and figured out, we rarely do. Human nature, thankfully, is to go full speed ahead and do what we *have* to do. It is all the more pleasant if we make sure there are plenty of smiles and laughs along the way, of course. I once gave the dirtiest blowout diaper *ever* to my father when he was visiting. Not to pass the buck, though it was a nice perk, but for the video camera to catch his reaction when he discovered the mess. Life works itself out, it always does. Not knowing what is around the bend keeps us traveling around that bend. If we cherish the laughable moments and choose to grin and shrug when the unexpected happens, the percent errors carry very little weight. Now, so many years later, we cannot imagine a life without twin boys and have decidedly come to realize there is a reason God presents us with so many unknowns. We might have been too fearful to take the leap or too busy to accept the responsibilities, and what a different future that would have given us. No, I choose to forge ahead into the unknown and scary thing that is Life, fully realizing that there will be surprises I am unaware of, sadness I cannot foresee, but also moments of beauty I cannot even fathom. Travel with me.

chapter two

she's having a puppy

Prior to our dive into parenthood, life was what I would call...simple. The house was quiet, conducive to being a student studying into the wee hours of the night. Brandon was a good husband, home for dinner each night, eager to spend entire weekends together exploring Atlanta or just fixing up the house. From the moment we were married however, I wanted to extend the family and having waited *seven years* to marry the man, my patience was running thin. My darling husband (well versed by the "new-husband guidelines" that I am certain exist) decided to follow this unwritten yet well-known rule for newlyweds:

When your new wife asks for a baby, get her a dog.

(FYI, I got *two* dogs in the course of our first three years of marriage.)

The premise of course is that the wife will have something to take care of and nurture while the husband will have a few more years of sleep and sex. (The latter ranking highest on new husband priorities, of course.) Admittedly, there is some truth to all of this. Puppies have those enormously sad eyes that plead for us to pick them up. Their skin is warm, wrinkly and full, smooth as a baby's bottom. And with the right puppy shampoo you can even make them smell like talcum powder. Most women cannot resist them.

The acquisition of a puppy is actually quite brilliant, putting off the many responsibilities that an *actual baby* presents while honoring some of our own maternal instincts to nurture. Puppies may cry out at night, true, but a puppy in the bed is far less hassle than diaper changes and breastfeeding until dawn. Puppies can be expensive, admittedly, but the purchase of a crate, some chew toys and a bag of dog food won't break your bank account like your first run to Babies R' Us will. Furthermore, the undeniable, unconditional love those puppies have for you from the moment you choose *them* at the shelter, warms even the coldest of hearts.

The perk for us newlyweds, of course, is that even after the pup has taken up residence in our home there is still time for those fun, flirty moments with our loved one. We are less apt to be drop-dead tired at the end of a day being a dog owner than if we were a baby owner. The mere suggestion of bedtime recreation in a doggy-ridden home has not yet been labeled absurd, as in the hypothetical household down the street where Jane is nursing a newborn while Jack is dreaming of breasts divinely designed for the sole enjoyment of men and not offspring. It is astonishing, really, to remember the days pre-children when you decided on Saturday morning that a hike would be fun and five minutes later, you are *actually* hiking. A leash and your own shoes completed the packing list. Jack and Jane, in contrast, are still busy packing bottles, bibs, blankets, wipes, diapers, diaper cream, pacifiers, bonnets, sunscreen, bug spray, stroller, stroller appropriate toys, band-aids, thermometer, baby Tylenol, baby Benadryl, and a cell phone for emergency aid should the baby fall out of the stroller because Daddy wasn't paying attention. I remember when there was no need to schedule a date night because *every night* was a potential date night. Dinner out? Let's go! Want to catch a movie? Sure! The ice-cream shop at 10:00 PM? Why not! Hey, bring the dogs!

Did dog ownership prepare me for parenthood? Absolutely not. Not even close. Keep in mind we were those obsessive (and *fantastic*, my dogs would assert) dog owners who took our dogs *everywhere.* We took them to the drive-in theater, the campsite, and to the beach. If it was their birthday, we took them to Dairy Queen for their own soft serve cone. We loved those animals as if they were our children. We took them on our fifteen-hour drives home to Wisconsin to see family three times a year - much to our parent's dismay, I might add. Our two-door Honda Civic carried us over eight hundred miles with the windows rolled down and two sixty pound monsters in the back seat with drool flying. I have wonderful memories of my first dog, Tyson, enjoying his first snowfall on one of those trips, tip-toeing his way through the snow and eating it by the mouthfuls. (This was our mistake, as we were pulling over every hour after that so he could relieve his bladder.) We had sledding excursions at the local water tower hill with those big furry lugs pulling our nieces and nephews down the slippery slope. I remember one particularly long and tedious drive home when even music blaring and icy air conditioning could not keep us awake. We were forced to pull over at a rest stop to get some shuteye and when we woke up a few hours later, I discovered

Oakley breathing so heavy that the windows of the car were completely fogged and my pillow was damp from his slobber. There was no complaining from us though. We started our morning with good hearty laughs and they started theirs with solid pats on their heads. God, we loved those dogs.

Humor me while I make a confession though: *loving them was not always easy.* There were days when my finger wagging due to poor pooch behavior actually made my hands ache and days when I tossed those pups into their kennel, slammed the gate, and walked out my front door. There were afternoons when I had tears streaming down my face after finding my eighty-dollar textbooks in shreds all over my living room. We cringe when we recall the (now-embarrassing) conversations between my husband and I that included admissions of possible mistakes in the puppy-selection task. On those particular days we would find ourselves wondering why in God's name we had dogs.

Tyson was our first pup and the true test of potty training a very young puppy. He was a clever little thing too, quickly learning that if he peed in *one spot*, we found the puddle and his nose was about to meet the puddle. Rather than asking to be put outside however, he came up with the crazy notion of emptying his bladder *while walking,* leaving little drips of urine in crazy figure eights and spirals all over our bedroom floor that would often go undiscovered until the next morning. It took one of our own necessary middle-of-the-night runs to the bathroom, our feet oddly wet during the trip, to figure out the method to his madness. Let me just add that it is a lot harder to clean up eight hundred little dribbles than it is to clean up one rather large puddle. That was the night in our puppy rearing life that the little things stopped bothering us. No longer did we mind his audacity to sleep on our couch or chew up our pens. Those things were deemed harmless and a lot less messy than the potty training hell we were in. Puppy proofing the house, we decided, was just a necessary evil in dog ownership. Loving our dog came with a price, and if Home Depot made a lot of money that year in the name of the Hellenbrand family loving their animal, so be it.

Enter, Oakley, the yellow lab that I had always dreamed of having. This was before the Marley & Me bestselling book and movie, by the way. It turns out that I was just a few years too slow telling my story. Oakley was what graced our home after I asked (the second time) to have a baby. Both of our dogs were rescue dogs from the

Atlanta Humane Society, our Oakley being part yellow lab and part something else. All shelters, if there is even an inkling of Labrador breeding in them, will label a dog "part Lab." What they do not tell you is what the other half might be. The "something else," the other fifty percent in Oakley's case was the breed I call Trouble. But my, oh my, was he beautiful. Big floppy ears, a coat like buttermilk, and a spotted tongue that hung practically to the floor when he was happy, Oakley was a sixty-pound lap dog, nap dog, watch-out-the-window-when-you-leave dog. He was also Alpha Dog. In his mind we were just renting space on Chaucer Place Road, not actually paying the mortgage. Tyson was never really too thrilled with our new acquisition, but he slowly came to tolerate him. He graciously allowed Oakley to run the show. Without Tyson ever really knowing it (and certainly he would never admit it), the two dogs slowly became friends. I now recognize it as a strategic step in the Who is the Best Dog Game, however. In comparison to Oakley, who was *always* getting into trouble, Tyson looked like an angel.

There are some pretty memorable casualties during Oakley's puppyhood. A Houdini escape from the puppy kennel left wire spokes scattered around the room and a hole in the floor. Textbooks were again a favorite, the binding was so chewy and gluey and irresistible that I decided it was just about time to finally graduate and shelve those books for good. The Lawn Furniture Incident takes the cake though. We wrongly assumed that the backyard was indestructible. It was a decent sized yard, fully fenced, with both a sunny patch of grassy heaven for lazy doggy lounging and a densely wooded space for rambunctious frolics with various woodland animals. We humans had a small space we called our own with a table, some chairs, an umbrella, and a grill for time spent with friends within our own genus and species. Sounds just right for two dogs and their cohabitating human pets, right? Well, let us just say that the umbrella took the brunt of Oakley's anxieties that particular day. And when the lawn furniture was all in pieces, and the woodland creatures had all been run off, Oakley decided to jump the reinforced eight-foot fence and go looking for us. That started his long running trend to escape and explore the wide, wide world. He always came back, God bless him.

Actually, God blessed our little family to the point that we all came to appreciate and accept each other as only a good family can. We loved our pups when they licked our feet and when they curled up next to us for a movie night. We loved them when they joined us on excursions into Atlanta and blurred our windows with their slobber. We loved them when they tirelessly met us at the door upon returning from work or school, always with a chew toy ready in their mouth for a lively game of fetch. We loved them when they raced around the living room at *mach speed* right before bed and then crashed on their pillows with an audible sigh. We loved them when they greeted our twin baby boys for the first time, with curious wet noses and licks of love on baby toes. When our boys squeaked and chirped, just days old and only four pounds each, we loved that Oakley came running to the bed to peer at them with wonder, his entire backside waving from side to side. We loved our big ole' pups as if they *were* our kids.

Fast-forward a year and half. Brandon and I are so caught up with teaching our twin boys to walk that we do not realize the dogs have not been walked in *weeks*. Oh, they still got their exercise. We had almost an acre of land by then, and we took them out back every day for some romping around. They still got their pats on the head, treats for tricks, and belly rubs, if a little less frequent. Of the two dogs, Tyson was the one that noticed the change in priorities a new family with children inherently undergo. He was the one that I would find looking at us from across the room with a look of angst in his eyes, probably remembering The Good Times. Gone were the days of the dogs being the recipients of my incessant chattering or Daddy's need for some rough housing. But bless their hearts, those puppies of mine waited patiently while we ourselves came into parenthood. They still met us at the door every evening and they still kissed my little boys while being crawled over, pulled on, or even hooked up to wagons like mules. Oakley still chased flashlights on the wall with as much vigor as ever, and Tyson still crawled up on the couch after the house was quiet and the kids were down to bed. It was a new normal for us and the dogs still brought joy to our ever-changing lives.

It was June 12, 2005 when Oakley was brought home to me in a pickup truck. A kind neighbor found him down the street, suffering from internal injuries after being hit by a car. Oakley had escaped the night before through a three-foot gap in our new fence. My husband was going to finish the fence, literally, the next day. It was one day too late. Oakley bolted after a rabbit in full Oakley-form, oblivious to our pleading to stop running and return home. I spent hours that night driving through the nearby neighborhoods yelling his name and watching for a large yellow streak to go by. Around three o'clock that morning I resolved myself to wait until the first light of morning to head out again. He always came home after his wild escapades, and I figured that he must have been disoriented in the dark and the sun would help him find his way home. I was right. He was hit while running back into our neighborhood that morning sometime just before the seven o'clock hour. He did not make it to our front door where I had left the door open with a hot dog on the front step. I never got to hear his whine for water, rest and a pat on the head. Instead we got a phone call from a gentleman telling us he had our dog. While I was grabbing a leash out of the laundry room, smiling from ear to ear at Brandon, I happened to hear over the speakerphone "dead dog." That was when I started sobbing.

My husband carried Oakley out of the pickup truck and laid him in a soft grassy spot in our backyard. There was no blood or gruesome mess and at first glance he looked as perfect as ever. An awkward angle to his backside suggested he had been struck there with his lumbar vertebrae most likely fractured. He died of internal bleeding, I suppose. While my husband was handling the logistics of it all, taking our boys to the neighbors, and getting ready to dig a hole in the backyard for one of our best friends, I just sat on a patch of green lawn and stroked Oakley's body. And I talked to him. I told him all the things about him that I loved. I told him all the things that drove me crazy. I told him that I would miss all of it. At some point in my musings Tyson came over, sniffed around and acted genuinely confused as to why the big lug did not get up and greet him back. At that point I remember taking off Oakley's dog tag and requesting a blanket to wrap around him so he would be warm when we buried him. Brandon also gathered Oakley's favorite bone and toy, a squeaky orange thing that could keep him running for hours, and tried to prepare me for the necessary step of saying a final goodbye.

I was not ready. I needed more time. It all seemed so unfair. If I had kept looking for him the night before, could we have avoided this? If we had finished that fence last night instead of hanging out with some friends, would my Oakley still be alive? I laid my head on that big dog's chest for one last hard cry. My own chest heaved while my tears ran over his fur. I laid there like that for what seemed like an eternity. It was while I was resting on him, not even capable of contemplating life without his happy soul in it, that he let out his last breath. A deep, long sigh that actually caused my head to sink with him. It was so profound and for a brief moment my heart leapt, thinking my prayers were answered and he was not dead after all. But no, he was gone. He simply granted me that last breath, allowing me to believe he had just heard me pour my heart out to him and he knew how much we would miss him.

There is a yellow stone the exact color of Oakley's fur that marks his final resting place in our backyard. I love that stone because when I miss him, I can look out the window and almost see him sitting out there curled up taking a nap. It is three years later that I am writing this and I am brought to sobbing tears while sitting with my laptop at a coffee shop. That troublesome, crazy, *lovely* dog was the closest, most important thing I have ever lost in this world. There is a 16 x 20 inch charcoal rendition of both of my dogs that hangs in our living room, an anniversary present to my husband in 2003. It is priceless to me. Oakley's dog tag sits on that frame, and one day Tyson's will as well.

Yes, having dogs and having kids is different. Raising my dogs did not begin to prepare me for raising my children. Dogs do not have grumpy days or their own agendas, and they rarely sass back. Their needs are simple, being quite satisfied with the basics of food, shelter and frequent tummy rubs, while my children require…we will just say *more*. However, at the end of the day I believe that loving them is pretty much the same. If you give them everything you have, even a dog can reside very strongly in your heart. Losing that piece of your heart leaves an empty hole that can never be replaced. Thankfully, our children can distract us from that hole. They keep the laughter in the household going, even through the sadness. The kids continue to greet us at the door when Oakley no longer can. Every time I come home and see the smiles on my children's faces, and Tyson's tail wagging, pleading to be played with, I am reminded of a big yellow dog who stole my heart and taught me that loving is what life is all about.

chapter three

all the dinosaurs are dead?!?

A couple of years later, and a third baby later, I am in the thick of my Slowing Down Project. It does not always go well. There are days when I am clearly Marlin-esque in my approach to parenting and others when I find it possible to exhibit just a little bit of Dory's nonchalance. On my good days I step over the pile of dirty laundry, skirt past the dirty dishes and play with abandon. We pull out the paint sets, the Legos, or we head to the park for a day in the sun. One of our favorite stops is the local Atlanta Bread Co. for a mid-morning snack, hence why my children refer to the place as "Muffins & Bagels." We may play a board game there after our tummies are full or simply chat about the goings-on of our family. Usually someone in the grandmother/grandfather age group comes up to me during our snack to tell me what well-mannered, darling children I have. I smile a proud mommy smile and continue to sip my coffee, feeling like I just scored a slam-dunk. I admit that I am proud of them at those moments and even a little proud of myself as well. These little dates to Muffins & Bagels will go down as some of the sweetest memories I have with them. Their faces covered in powdered sugar, three sets of little legs swinging under the table while they find room in their tummies for yet another bite. It is truly precious.

If I was not already attempting to record my children's lives within the chapters of this book, the tidbits I share with you here would exist in some other form. I have an antique chifferobe in my bedroom that serves as a memory keeper of sorts, the antique key serving as a very effective sentry from curious rummaging by four-year-old hands. Each of my children have a drawer within the chest dedicated to their keepsakes ranging from casts from broken arms (stinky!), unique artwork and even their first locks of hair. On either side of the drawers are locked cabinet doors that swing open to a closet containing all of my children's cutest baby clothes, christening gowns, and hand-painted t-shirts that still smell like baby powder, or even the salty beach at which they were worn. Resting at the bottom of each locked cupboard lie their baby books stuffed to the brim with photos not yet posted within, and stacks of Post-It notes with first words, funny toddler-esque expressions or other memorable moments. To this day, whenever I here the word "spider," my brain hears "swiber" and even inserts one of those little smiley face emoticons after it. We will call it tissue memory. ☺ It is one of the most pleasantly sweet rewards of parenthood, these silly little things that come out of our children's mouths.

This chapter epitomizes the beauty of motherhood: the funny stuff, the adorable stuff, and the moments that you never get back no matter how much you wish for it. These are the occasions that my children did or said *something* that engraved itself upon my heart and I want to share it. In the current times, I might have just posted it on my Facebook page, or twittered it. I, however, want my children to have a hard copy of these memories. When these moments of beauty happen something innately tells us that we may only get to experience this particular act of cuteness once (or if we're lucky, twice) before our little one inevitably turns into a (brace yourself) *teenager*. True, some families skirt around this sad yet simple truth by simply having *more* children. Some of them eventually have so many of these little munchkins that everyone gawks at them because there are *seven* little ones to keep track of. I suspect that they *just cannot help it.* The innocence and candor that surround our children, almost resembling an aura, is a lifeline in an otherwise crazy and chaotic world.

Our lives as mothers are filled with these sweet spots (or happy places) that seem to fuel our gas tanks and keep us emotionally steady and fulfilled on this journey. My son Tristan, inevitably at least once each day, belts out in his best party voice, *"Everybody dance now! Doo! Doo-doo-doo-doo!"* From there he begins his break-dancing body shakes, imitating the dancing turkey from the Shrek Christmas special. I watch him with wonder (white boys *cannot* dance), my eyes roll and they meet my husband's. We cannot help but grin from ear to ear. Moments like these are not the mandatory ingredients in the recipe of our family life, or even vital components that keep my family clothed, fed and kept safe. No, but they are the added spice to an otherwise boring recipe. They are the icing and sprinkles on our life's cupcake. Think of these little shared moments with *your* family as the whipped cream on a good mug of hot chocolate. Not mandatory, but cause for grin.

Of course, we can get through the business of life without jotting these things down and on some days, it is easy to not even notice them. In my opinion it is the days I *do not* notice or appreciate the small blessings that are my "off" days. The days when the *business* of being a mother runs over and kills the *experience* of being a mother. In reality there are days when I do not even *see* my children. I might cook them breakfast and get them dressed and maybe even sit down and play a game of checkers with them, but still not really *look at them.* My mind might be hovering in a misty cloud of responsibilities (or just be in dire need of a nap), where it seems I observe these beautiful little people from afar. This happened quite frequently when my boys were infants and early toddlers. I owned my own chiropractic office then, working part-time at the practice and spending the remaining portion of my days at home. When people asked, I told them I had the best of both worlds. The truth, however, was not so pretty. Compartmentalizing my life in that way never really worked for me. While at home I was commonly thinking of work and when I was at my office, I was wishing *I* was the one teaching my kids their colors rather than my perfectly wonderful nanny. When I stopped to examine why I felt so overwhelmed all the time, why I felt such a longing to run away from Georgia and move back to my home state of Wisconsin, I realized that my life was not at all balanced. In fact, in was grossly off kilter. At any given time it felt like I was driving with only two tires on the road. I may have been labeled Super Mom by others, but at the end of the day *none* of it was my *best work.* It was purely survival mode, and it was exhausting.

Selling my chiropractic office was a blessing, in more ways than one. Having built my office from scratch, I was proud to have built a practice where I was seeing between eighty to one hundred patients per week. On the downside, I was dog-tired. Any entrepreneur knows that having your doors open for twenty-five hours per week translates into a forty to fifty hour workweek. The behind-the-scenes brainstorming, marketing and required maintenance of a professional office was profound. When I found out to my surprise that I was pregnant with Baby Number Three, (my twins were not even two years old yet) I began to earnestly look for the window with which to bolt from. Life felt like a spinning tilt-a-whirl ride at Six Flags, and I was desperate for a puke bucket. The chiropractor I found to cover for me while I was laid up sick with pregnancy-induced nausea was a former classmate of mine. She kept my practice afloat and in the end she purchased my practice from me. Most practices are on the market for two years before a buyer comes along. In six short weeks I was able to hop off that tilt-a-whirl ride, steady myself for the first time with all four wheels on the road and try my skills at full time mommyhood.

Years later I still have weekly work meetings, they are just over Chick-fil-A chicken nuggets, my staff consisting of two wily four-year-olds and an easy-to-please two-year-old. Accounting these days finds me budgeting in bribery money for good behavior, and patient care involves regular chiropractic adjustments for my own little ones to ward off those snotty noses the rest of the kids at the park have. The best perk of my new job is that I find myself noticing and appreciating my children more. I notice the brilliant blue, almost hazy look in Tristan's eyes when he is dreaming up exactly *how* to turn the pile of recyclables in front of him into an elevator for his dinosaurs. I pause to watch little Brooklynn gaze up to heaven while she searches her brain for the name of that color I am asking her to identify. Granted, a photograph might capture the brilliant blue, or even the heavenward gaze, but in most cases the essence of the moment, the emotional experience leading us to take the picture in the first place, is lost. How often have you looked at a picture you took on your camera and thought, "Now what were we doing here? What brought about this expression of awe or puzzlement that is painted on my child's face?" The phenomenon of scrapbooking our memories has become so popular lately because it allows us to weld together – permanently, or as long as the acid-free paper will allow – the images of our children *with* the written words of emotion that accompanied the moment. A sticky note on the back of a photo thrown in a shoebox at the back of our closet is not as satisfying. I find that the most meaningful photographs of my children have a story behind them. For example, standing behind their Papa Roger's house deep in southern Montana, wading through ankle deep weeds aside a rapidly moving, ice-cold creek, my twin boys *simultaneously* dropped their drawers to the ground and took a leak together. It is my father's hearty chuckle at this backyard scene (almost reminiscent of a Santa Claus chortle) that would have been lost in only a photograph of our afternoon.

Pausing long enough to not only witness but also *experience* these moments has shown me how precious each day really is. There was a period of time in our recent past when my little Tristan was laying in a hospital bed, his body wracked by a temperature of 106.1 with the doctors clueless as to why. Brain damage has been documented at temperatures around 104 degrees, so I admittedly was terrified. Given that the doctors could not find the source of the infection that was obviously wrecking havoc in my son's body, I began to wonder if I would get to see my child grow into a six-year-old, ten-year-old, or teenager. Or if he did survive this ordeal, I worried I might not have another conversation with him about his beloved orca whales, beluga whales, great white sharks and the like. That was the scariest time in my life, thinking I might lose a piece of what makes Tristan uniquely "Tristan." To this day, the smell of antiseptics or even hearing the cartoon Sponge Bob, takes me back to those perilous days spent in the Pensacola Sacred Heart Children's Hospital. My mind's eye sees myself wrapped around his tiny little body on that hospital bed, praying the rosary for the first time in many, many years while my slowly healing and recovering son quietly laughs at something that ridiculous cartoon sponge just said. I can instantly bring back the bright white spot of kidney calcification discovered on the ultrasound monitor five days after entering their doors, suggesting an unchecked kidney infection and therefore the necessary antibiotics to treat it. I have read that a strong smell or other sensory stimulation at the precise moment in which a trauma occurs, can years later take you right back to that moment. Those memories of our hospital stay are some I wish I could surgically excise out of my gray matter and toss in the medical waste trash can. But no, life is not that clean and neat. We cannot choose what we remember, only how much weight we give it. The power that memory has to pick me up and carry me away each time one of my children has a fever is ludicrous and yet in the same token needs to be honored. Fighting it outright only makes me feel more out of control.

Happily, I can report many other smells or sounds that bring back moments of pure pleasure. My son Blake adores having the palms of his hands and his fingers stroked. The incense in church the other day coupled with simply having him close by brought back a memory of a long forgotten Sunday when he was having an especially hard time sitting still for mass. He was suffering from a severe case of the wiggles and giggles, and I honestly thought we were doomed to the nursery. But he looked up at me, gave a slight nod and a tip of his head, and eloquently placed his hand in mine. I gently traced my index finger along the bones of his hand and immediately saw his legs go limp and his head fall into my side. Whether or not the scent of incense will pass directly to his limbic system and bring back that memory, I do not have the foggiest notion. I cherish that neural pathway, however. Another such memory, tied to my cochlear nerve this time, features my husband and daughter. I do not believe I will ever hear Taylor Swift sing her country hit "Tim McGraw" without seeing in my mind's eye Brandon holding Brooklynn in his arms, spinning her around in the living room with her blond hair flying, squeals of delight filling the house. The look on Brandon's face while he's spinning her around is what heaven on this earth would look like. I am sure of it.

Memory is a tricky thing and I will not pretend to understand it. The reason that one funny toddler dictionary entry sticks in my head while so many others have long been deleted from my memory banks is unexplainable. A couple of our personal Parent-Revised Webster Dictionary entries include:

> Boogies: (noun) particles found deep within the nose of a child that most grown adults feel (quite strongly) should stay there
>
> Cutecumber: (noun) late spring vegetable commonly sown and grown by industrious children because they are so darn cute (and tasty, I might add)

Brooklynn was a late talker, not saying much until she was well over two years old. It was very difficult to understand her chattering at times, and even more frustrating for those of us around her because she made it *crystal* clear how important her words were by the way she said them so deliberately and with such conviction. I will never forget when I finally figured out what my little girl was referring to when she so gleefully talked about the "ho-ho." Being that my child had never laid eyes on Little Debbie snack cakes, I assumed she was not referencing a desired afternoon treat. No, in her mind a dog does not say "woof" or "ruff" or anything else I have ever read in a children's book as dog lingo. A dog says "ho-ho" and you best remember it. Of course even after parents correct the misnomer children tend to hold onto them for good ole' posterity's sake. The first time I explained that "narbles" are actually *marbles* the boys looked at me as if I had just suggested that up was actually down. So years later, I have accepted that cutecumbers still grow in my garden, because they are still *cute* and what is "cuc" anyway?? It reminds me of how I feel when I have been singing a favorite song repeatedly, sometimes for *years* and then one day someone hears me and tells me I have the words wrong. *What? Are you kidding me?* I have found that it can actually ruin the song. I am sure this is how they felt when I had to break the news to them that those whales they have been in love with for about *three years* are not actually huNKback whales, but huMPback whales. In all honesty I felt terrible about this late discovery of a completely technical point. I wish I could have told them sooner. Apparently I never listened well enough to decipher the pronunciation they were using. I did not know they were even in error until Blake read a show on TV about humpback whales and started laughing that the TV spelled it wrong. Though *he* ultimately took it well, Tristan looked at me as if I had morphed into a little green Martian right there in the living room. To this day I am not certain he feels comfortable with the proper name of this magnificent ocean animal that he adores and knows *everything* about. "They have baleen not teeth, Mom. And two blowholes, not one. Oh, and they eat krill, are warm-blooded and they are not fish." He additionally now knows they have humpy backs not hunky ones. I hope I did not ruin it for him.

Kids are adorably literal at this age. A "cutecumber" had better be cute and a crack on the sidewalk could lay you up for days if you step on it. Our commonly used expressions are beyond their little child brains, either ignored or just missed altogether - much to the delight of Pixar Entertainment. There is a children's book that I have read to my kids for years, I Love You All the Time. I love the message and we actually sing the words so it is a favorite for all of us. The lesson I have learned from the book however, is different from the one my children learned. They use it as their Ace card in the event they have just committed a crime and I happen to be quite angry with them. "But Mama…You love me all the time…" The bomb squad just defused Mama. Of course, "literal" only *begins* to explain their view of the world. If you tell them that monster spray (AKA water spritzer) will keep the monsters away at night, they want to know where the monsters go when you spray them. If you tell them that they have bunnies in their ears that must be extracted with Q-tips, then they want to see more than just remnants of carrots on those dirty Q-tips. And besides, how do bunnies fit in there?!? When you tell them there are dust bunnies under their beds, they feel overrun by bunnies and want to know how bunnies got in the house in the first place. So the day that I told the kids we were going to a museum to see dinosaurs, I should have been prepared for the conversation that came next.

We had read books about dinosaurs together, watched The Land Before Time movie and knew the difference between "long necks" and "sharp teeth" dinosaurs. My boys have a few dinosaur toys, both big and small, and we had played on many occasions with the roaring, stomping replicas. They knew that fossils were old dinosaur bones buried in the dirt and they even got good at piecing together dinosaur skeletons with various puzzles and such. They knew that some were meat eaters and some only ate plants. And they even got to see some awesome exhibits at the Museum of Natural History in Chicago during a previous visit home. On this particular morning we were all loaded up in the car for our fieldtrip to the Fernbank Museum in Atlanta, to see the dinosaurs. Their excitement was palpable, their legs kicking in their car seats, dinosaur toys in their laps. I am pulling out of the driveway when Tristan says, "Mama, will we get to see the dinosaurs awake or will they all be sleeping?" Huh? Pause. Cue the crickets chirping. I eventually put the car back into park, turned back to look at them with puzzlement and a face that suggested *they* were aliens this time. "The dinosaurs are dead, guys" was my answer. I know…real sympathetic right? This was the point when tears poured down their cheeks like California mudslides. Tristan, with outright terror on his face exclaimed, "*All* the dinosaurs are dead?" OMG.

First I feel frustration. "Well, of course they are all dead, guys!" Then I feel sadness for the boys, their tears are numerous and heartbreaking to witness. I try to console them, crawling into the backseat of the car to give them hugs and dry their tear-stained cheeks. Once they are relatively calm I climb back into the driver's seat. This is when I begin to feel embarrassment and a tiny sense of disappointment in myself. I let them down. Not only was I curt in my initial response to them, but I somehow managed to teach them everything about dinosaurs *except* that every single dinosaur in the entire world has been dead for a million bazillion years. And I am not very proud of myself for it. Well, I will say this much, I will not forget again. Give me another little four-year-old dinosaur-loving boy and he will be well versed on extinction, because those tears in the back seat were *real.* Children are so trusting of our world, so hopeful and literal and precious all at the same time. They trust us, their parents, more than anyone in this world to protect them. They trust us for accurate information, for safety, for unconditional love. When we fail to provide those things we can find ourselves doubting our abilities as parents.

Of course, we are often too hard on ourselves because there is no such thing as a perfect parent, in the same way there is no such thing as a perfect child. If we deem them perfect, it is only because we accept them as they are and overlook their faults. In the same way that they trust us with abandon, we must trust ourselves. We must trust that our imperfect parenting still brings about beautiful results. So in the end, all of the time we spend together need not be perfect. It is not necessary for me to be proud of them in order to support and love them. It is not necessary for me to be a perfect mother in order for them to feel unconditional love. Remembering and recounting the perfect moments with our children, when we smiled and were proud of them, is quite enjoyable. However, we also must learn to give credence to the imperfect moments when we bruised their souls a little, did not give enough of ourselves or beat ourselves up because we made a mistake. I suspect that when all is said and done it will not matter how perfectly I did my job, or how perfectly they did theirs, it will only matter that we did it together.

chapter four

mean mommy

Yesterday was one of *those* mornings. You know the kind I mean: when you hit the snooze button one too many times and then with a shudder of realization know you have only fifteen minutes to get yourself ready for the day. The kids will need me at six o'clock sharp to rouse them from their slumber so that they can begin the awesome task of dressing, teeth brushing, breakfast and packing their school bags. (Oh, and shoes. Never forget to factor in time for shoes.) So figuring I need about five minutes to start the coffee pot while throwing a few dishes from last night into the dishwasher, and then thirty seconds to slam down a shot of caffeine to enable the hyper-alert state necessary for all of us to be out the door in time for school, I am left with only nine and half minutes for my own hygiene and attire. This late start to the day has guaranteed that my shower (which provides otherwise childless people a state of cleanliness that, alas, has become optional for me over the past six years) will have to be skipped this morning in favor of cooking breakfast for my children. Yes, mothers make these self-sacrifices on a daily basis in the name of their children.

In case you were wondering, yes – we actually did make it out the door this morning. And no, I did not have to do the walk of shame through the school hallways, sharing sympathetic glances with the other parents whom also found this morning more than they could handle, resulting in a tardy status for their pupils. We successfully got out the door, got in our car, drove across town through traffic, and drove through the drop off line to our desired destination. We just happen to have accomplished it with a lot of yelling, growling, stomping, steam blowing, and tears the size of golf balls streaming down our cheeks. I would like to add that tears that large on a four-year old are actually quite astonishing to see. And they are quite distressing to a Mama that just elicited them. Enter, Mean Mommy.

Most of you are actually assuming that Mean Mommy is the nickname my children assigned to me that morning upon discovering the un-showered, too-little-caffeinated, multi-tasking gorilla that they woke to that morning. In reality, it is the nickname I labeled *myself* with in order to get their little bottoms a-movin' that day. It was yet another one of those sometimes effective, yet in all likelihood socially unacceptable means of rallying the troops to accomplish a necessary task. Some of you may know it under its more common name, otherwise known as *a threat*. ("You better or else…If you don't, I'll…" and similar expletives usually used by a parent during one of their finer parental moments.) I believe that a *bribe* also falls into this same category of parental tools, condemned in public by the same parents that use them in private. So I believe I am about to share with you one of my most shameful moments as a parent and admit that these words actually came out of my mouth: "If you boys don't start listening to me and get ready for school, I will be Mean Mommy today. Do you want me to be Mean Mommy today?" You can imagine their look of shock and horror when I am confirming that in fact *there is* a Mean Mommy that can be set loose in the house. We have just had confirmation folks that in fact it was *not* their imagination that sometimes the very mommy that loves them dearly and would do just about anything in the name of their happiness can actually morph into a creature of…*meanness*. At this point I will hang my head in disgrace while you nod affirmatively that you have been in the same boat. At least in the same body of water. At least once? Maybe?

Oh, and to make matters worse this particular threat did *not* actually work to get them out the door faster. Big surprise, huh? Instead, as you can imagine, it only created a far louder and toxic environment in which to escape from. So why do we do this? I'm fairly certain that nine times out of ten - okay ninety nine times out of one hundred – the children subjected to a Mean Mommy (or Mean Daddy) are probably really only guilty of having not slept long enough for respective Mommy or Daddy to *get a grip on it*. Apparently I did not grip the horns of that bull I woke up on yesterday and tell it in so many words, *whoa boy*. I allowed, instead for a full out Spanish bull-run to occur right there in my own living room and it so happened that we *all* got tossed right over the fence in consequence.

After the worst of it was over, while driving them all to school in a very quiet and sad little caravan, I paused long enough to assess the broken pieces of our morning. Though I am eternally ashamed of my behavior, I can with some nominal amount of pride tell you that I *sincerely* apologized to those little people of mine. I apologized that I yelled, stomped and generally acted like the bull I felt that I was riding at the time. I apologized that I chased them out of the house like a fox chasing chickens out of a hen house. I apologized that there *even was* such a distinction of Mean Mommy within the woman that stands before them as the receiver of the little blessings that are my children. Thank goodness my little people are so forgiving, I might add. With hugs and kisses and a heart-felt pat on my back from Tristan, they told me it was all right and that sometimes even mommies make mistakes. "Right, Mom......?" asked Blake. This is a loaded question because I know without a doubt that this moment of humility will come back up the next time I am setting rules or standards for behavior in my home. Quite possibly, they will be thinking, *Mommy is probably wrong again...*But I nodded my head and replied, that "Yes, baby. Even mommies make mistakes."

Though days like the one described above are painful and formidable, they can also be valuable. I am slowly coming to realize that while my goal as a parent is to guide my children to become intelligent, compassionate and respectful people, my children are concomitantly teaching me some valuable life lessons as well. If I choose to ignore their own brand of wisdom and instead force upon them My Way or the Highway, it may leave me standing on the side of the road by myself. The open road would probably look amazingly appealing after a morning spent with Mean Mommy, after all.

Looking back, there are several moments in my life when I can honestly pinpoint an event, written passage, or conversation when I knew without a doubt that I had just become wiser. There are not a lot of these moments, I am embarrassed to say. However, I cede that I am early in my journey, being a young thirty-two-year-old, and have a sneaky suspicion that there will be many more opportunities for wisdom. I would like to share with you a few of the moments when *my children's* astuteness was overwhelmingly necessary and much appreciated and concomitantly resulted in a wiser mother standing before them. I will warn you however that these...we will call them Learning Moments...often start off with me acting my *worst* and for that reason I do not particularly feel proud to be sharing them with you. However, were I to bow out and choose to sugarcoat them, this chapter would feel a farce, simply because these low moments in my life have created some of the most vivid and beautiful memories of my life with my children.

So here we go. Not so long ago, after a run of the mill difficult day with my kids, My Patience informed me it was running thin. It was one of those days when the lunch I made was "yucky" and the toys that filled their toy bins were "boring." It was when my to-do list was a mile long and my guilt for not playing constructively with the little monsters was even longer. They were mad at me and they were mad at each other. They were rude, obnoxious and way too loud. And when I finally had had enough and told them to get upstairs to their room for a Red Light (meaning a long and lonely time-out in their bed) they had the audacity to yell, "No!" That is when I snapped. I think I actually *chased* them up the stairs. (Well, right after I screamed loud enough that every child in our entire neighborhood knew to take cover.) I have to say that the method did accomplish what I wanted. I wanted them upstairs and far away from me. I wanted them to take a time-out, so that *I* could take a time-out.

About twenty minutes later after I had cooled down and found my head again, I went upstairs to their room. Neither of the boys was very happy with me, but they were not saying too much about it either. When I knelt down next to Blake's bed, he very quietly said, "My teacher never yells at us." I answered that statement with complete and utter silence. And then I said, "I know, and you are right, Blake. I am sorry." And then as I laid my head on his chest and listened to his breathing, something made me think of a Bible verse that the boys had memorized in the first few weeks of school. I had quizzed them on it for a full week and before that moment I really only knew it incompletely. But right then it came back to me in bold type clearness:

All have sinned and fall short of the glory of God. Romans 3:23

So we talked about that verse, and what it meant. And when I told him that I had sinned and was sorry for it, he simply said, "It's okay, Mom. I forgive you. And if you tell God you are sorry, He will forgive you too. My teacher told me that." What? Am I talking to Blake or did Yoda just walk into the room?

Blake has humbled me several other times since that particular day. On another occasion when he was grumpy, irritable and generally being difficult and I was at a loss for yet another directive to snap him out of it, he looked at me with that grumpy face, the smooth skin between his eyebrows all scrunched up and said, "Mom, I just need some lovin'." And so started the tickle and hug fest that scared those grumpies right out of him. To this day if I see him scowling or grumbling about one thing or another, I only have to ask him if he needs some lovin' and he grins at me and becomes something more pleasant in nature. Yet another reminder that no one is cheered up by an overbearing person commanding him or her to cheer up.

So…can I report that since becoming wiser I no longer yell at my children? Of course not. However, when I feel myself getting worked up by the kids and hear my voice rising or breaking with anger, Brooklynn and Tristan give me visual cues to their comfort level. Tristan will cover his ears. He might even close his eyes and I will instantly realize that I can tone it down some. And Brooklynn, poor Brooklynn, really only needs to be asked once, maybe twice in a volume acceptable in a *library,* to behave herself. Anything more than that can cause an all out breakdown and she will cry and tell me I hurt her feelings. Daddy has been a perpetrator of this crime against Brooklynn a few times as well, and I believe a part of his heart actually breaks when she gives him the consensus of the jury, "You hurt my feelings, Dada." It seems that as we become wiser as parents, we innately become quieter enforcers.

A few years ago, as a new mother, I sat up late one night with my in-laws discussing life and religion. These philosophical discussions commonly happen only after my hubby has fallen asleep on the couch, and have become more frequent in the past year. That particular night I told my in-laws that there was a part of the Catholic mass that I just did not agree with. Right before we accept communion the parishioners all say together, "Lord, I *am not* worthy to receive you, but only say the word and I shall be healed." I told them I did not agree. *I am worthy.* Isn't our God all-forgiving, after all? Didn't He make us in His own image? With free will to conduct ourselves in whatever manner we so choose? I might make mistakes and I might not be perfect, but darn it, I am worthy. I don't remember them really arguing with me about it or showing too much disappointment in my belief, but fast forward probably four years and three children later and let me tell you, *I am not worthy.* I may never be worthy. Thank goodness God loves me anyway. Thank goodness God already knew the day he created me that that I would be prone to yell a little too much and would suffer acute cases of impatience. *Thank goodness that He gave me these cute little munchkins anyway.*

Today, only twenty-four hours later, I can quite happily report that Mean Mommy did not rear her ugly head. There was no bull hiding under my covers incognito, though there might be one tomorrow that will need some firm taming and maybe a swift boot out the door. In the meantime, I can rest assured that today we started our day out right. Today we gave thanks for our food, thanks for our home, and thanks for barns to house those damn bulls in. We recognized that tears were not necessary, that stomping is not compulsory, and that the Spanish bull-run can be enjoyed via satellite. Now granted, a few Pokemon cards in the way of bribery might have aided in the swiftness of getting out the door this morning…but shhhh, that is just between us.

chapter five

hey Mom, those are cute panties you're wearing!

Blue jeans and a tank top, flip flops and painted toe nails is probably what you would find if you met me on the street. I once had a friend tell me that she knew I was her kind of girl because I rarely dress to impress. After judiciously and rather hurriedly reconsidering her statement, she looked at me and swore that was a compliment. Her assessment is accurate however. Nine days out of ten I find myself dressing sensibly in whatever outfit befits the goals for the day. Laundry day demands comfortable cotton, garden day means I wear whatever is already dirty on my floor. When I plan to work on this book or find myself with a scheduled coffee date with friends I tend to simply add a bracelet or nicer shoes to complement my jeans and t-shirt. Only for date nights, girls-night-out, or my infrequent marketing work for a fellow chiropractor do I find myself donning what others might consider "fashionable." Rarely do I need a drycleaner or an iron, a true blessing I think.

I stand five foot five inches on a good day, my face has a strong jaw line and my eyes change color depending on what I am wearing. I have a small frame with delicate bones, though I am usually hauling a thirty pound little girl around (she is the one with piggy tails and a thumb planted firmly in her mouth). Long, thick dishwater blond hair (thank you L'Oreal,) is easily the rationale for why I still discover my husband admiring me from afar even after we have been together for almost eighteen years. I have strong deltoids and biceps, almost unfairly, since they exist with little effort on my part, but they are the recipients of frequent stroking from my son Tristan while he sits contentedly next to me on the couch and so I will keep them.

As a reader of Joyce Meyer's books, her pages serving as a reminder to honor the strong woman I am regardless of whether my swimsuit fits properly, I still struggle with a poor self image that seems to plague more women I know than not. Quite frankly I find that honoring my children's imperfections (be it speech idiosyncrasies or an endlessly snotty nose) seems an easier task than honoring my own flaws. These little people are inherently cuter, softer, smoother and lovelier than their parent counterparts. An "outie" belly button is nothing but kissable on a toddler, but that same outie after childbirth just seems less endearing. I sometimes wish that my girlfriend Laura's It Is What It Is perspective could be tattooed on my forehead, and maybe on my backside, as a visual reminder each day to accept the body that God has given me and to stop coveting what he did not.

My sad, sordid history of poor body image is worth recounting and reflecting on if only because I am in the process of raising children whom I wish to have better self-image and self-confidence than I have. Where I feel compelled to worry about what everyone else thinks, I hope and dream for them to feel free to think for themselves. Of course this skill can not easily be learned in households where the opinions of children are not honored or even heard. Thinking for oneself, after all, comes with a price: endless debate. Debate over which park to frequent, which snack we should bring, which toy Blake wants even though Tristan currently has it in his possession are conversations we have daily *because I value and encourage them to tell me what they think.* Debating about whether it is too close to dinner time for an ice-cream snack or whether putting your toys away after playing is a reasonable responsibility for a four-year-old, have tied us up for ten minutes or more, with the four-year-olds commonly coming up with some surprisingly good arguments. The desire we have for our children to be strong and have a voice can come in direct conflict with the ease of daily activities in a home. The miserable truth for most parents is that our children's self-confidence will be largely determined while they are quite young and in my case became problematic the moment I was called Zit Face by a boy that I adored in fifth grade. Thankfully, twenty five years later I can proclaim with great happiness and relief that I am in possession of a very supportive husband who wouldn't dream of even mentioning a pimple the size of a volcano if it took up residence on my cheek. (And you know he darn well saw that thing.)

The wrinkles I have sown while living this life or the little pooch of fluff that sits on top of my belt (so lovingly planted there by my love for chocolate) does not define me. I am certain that if I got back into the gym next week I could burn that fluff right off, and a little Oil of Olay might smooth over a few harsh lines. One thing that cannot easily be airbrushed however is whether you love *yourself* unconditionally. So I teach my children how to defend their honor and their self-respect. A strong voice is one way. "Speak up and stand tall when the bully calls your name." A strong body is maybe another. "Fight back when they punch and punch harder than they did." In the quiet after the confrontations however, is when a confident person shines through. What does your inner voice say to you after you have been put down? Do you want to curl up into a ball and hide from the world? Or do you shrug your shoulders and say, "So what." How can I teach my children to love the person they are, the voice inside them, or even what they see in the mirror before some fifth grader viciously yanks their self-esteem from them?

I do not want to psychoanalyze all of the potential topics that could be psychoanalyzed regarding this topic. I recognize first and foremost that as a mother of a darling little girl, I best be getting more comfortable in my own skin so that she will be comfortable in hers. I must forgive the jeans that fit too tight, and forgive the muffin top that sits so lovingly on my hips. My son Blake, the ever sensible and goofy one, helps me on a daily basis put life into perspective. We had spent practically the entire summer at the beach, which can be tough for a recovering body-image freak. I was preparing myself for yet another afternoon at the pool, slipping my swimsuit on, when Blake exclaims, "Mom! Your butt is HUGE!" At which point all three of those little munchkins burst out into giggles. I was simultaneously appalled but laughing at the brutal honesty of a four-year-old. After all, his view from down there cannot be that flattering even for the most perfect derriere and at least he did not have the family camera in his possession this time. I shared this story with my husband that night, knowing he would find it funny. He does love it when I tell him the funny little things that he misses during the course of just another day in the Hellenbrand home. After a good chuckle, he kissed me on the top of my head, and with all seriousness reminded me that I am still his "Hotpants," a nickname he gave me when we were eighteen years old. Smiles, wifely eye rolling, and a monster-sized hug ensue.

I come to find out a few days later that my lovely husband has been busy instructing his two young boys in the etiquette of praising women for their physical features rather than exclaiming in loud voices the apparent *girth* of said features. Blake had apparently duly noted the lesson and proceeded to complement me on my "cute hiney" – his choice of words. I am not altogether certain that my four-year-old should be commenting *at all* on my backside, so he is clearly still a work-in-progress. Fast forward a few weeks and Blake gave me yet another compliment while standing with me in a dressing room at a department store. I was trying on new work clothes, a pile of discarded items vying for space on the bench with all three of my children. Now, I have to preempt this story by mentioning that Blake's favorite color is pink. (I know, I know, that could be an entirely different chapter in my book.) The fact remains that he still cannot figure out exactly why more boys do not like pink (it being a very complimenting color after all). So there I am, pulling up a pair of sleek, black trousers when my son decides to share with me *his* evaluation of this particular moment in time, "Hey, Mom! Those are cute panties you're wearing!" (They are pink, mind you.) I'm not sure what anyone else in that fitting room thought, how many spontaneous grins broke out on the population of women who were also shopping that day, listening to a four-year-old critique their mother on panty choice. I decided quite judiciously however, that I did look quite stunning in those pink panties. If I do say so myself.

Will my children grow up having a strong sense of self, really believing that what one carries inside is more important than what we display on the outside? I do not know. I can report that already my sweet little Brooklynn, crawling into bed with me in the morning, will often tell me I look beautiful in my dumpy t-shirt and frumpy sweatpants. (Even if she follows it up with a less favorable assessment of my breath.) Truthfulness comes so easily to little ones, tact less so. I believe that the sweetness of our greetings in the morning is where the true beauty lies. The cuddles, the hugs, the patience and love we show each other will be far more important than any physical attribute we were or were not blessed with. The strength we must summon when someone puts us down or tries to knock us over, or even something as simple as a mother reminding their child that they are in fact *good* and *kind* is really all that matters. I have high hopes that self-esteem grows from those simple yet thoughtful words and actions of a mother. Even if it comes from someone who smells like a raccoon died in her mouth.

chapter six

I'll find you first

As difficult as it is to be a mom, most of us are not doing this job alone. The man we chose to love and cherish is residing in our home, hopefully sleeping in our bed, and if we are *really* lucky he is helping us raise these genetic offspring we have sprung. I know fathers who are exemplary businessmen but sorely lack in the father category, while others who manage their nine-to-five job and still have the gumption to throw the kids in a bath before bed. Fathers come in as many colors and flavors as mothers do, and I suspect they have their own set of worries and woes as well. Putting food on the table, a roof over their family's head, along with a genuine desire to be home more and work less probably top most of their lists. Being that I do not myself have a pair of testicles however, I will not be so arrogant (or stupid) to discuss their trials and heartaches in this book. If Brandon chooses to write his own book one day entitled, The *Real* Happenings in the Hellenbrand Household I may discover that *my* reality is different from his own. Fascinating idea, however I am not holding my breath for his written version of our life. So I will hypothesize the possibilities, research the likely truths, but ultimately make the executive decision on what has been going on under our roof.

This take-charge mentality has been imprinted within my cells since the day I was born. I am a Capricorn after all, and though I'm not sure how much credence I put into the stars and horoscopes and mystical stuff, I do have twin boys that precisely fit the bill for a couple of party-animal Leos. What's more is that I do in fact seem to fit many of the characteristics of Capricorns. Almost terrifyingly well. First, I am inordinately stubborn and I am pretty sure that *I know it all*. Of course this was very frustrating for my mother while I was growing up since she never really agreed with the latter. It is true that I used to be able to argue my point until the sun goes down and though I am still *able* to, my husband usually exits the room shortly after I get started. Though I do love to hear myself talk I have found the practice to be quite unproductive and therefore have given it up. To some degree.

I am a perfectionist. I work best under pressure because otherwise I will edit and revise so many times I make a full circle and wind up right back where I started. I do not consider myself obsessive-compulsive about stuff but I take a lot of pride in what I do and try to accomplish my best. They say that many CEO's are Capricorns because we are intelligent, willing to work hard and are natural born leaders. I will take credit for having some pretty fantastic synapses in that brain of mine - or at least I used to. "Mommy Brain" has set in to some degree and consequently I have lost all ability to process numbers, dates, and the like. Occasionally I will have a conversation with someone that only a few days later I have no recollection of having, but I do have four years of professional school under my belt and I suppose you do not accomplish that without some brainpower.

Working hard is something that also comes natural to me. When I graduated from four years of chiropractic school (following four years attaining my Bachelor of Sciences degree), I had many options available to me. The most obvious option (and the most often chosen by new graduates) is to work for another doctor as an associate. Doing what might amount to grunt work for another doctor and being paid beans for it was not even an option for me, however. Being an independent contractor and essentially subleasing space from another doctor was another possibility, essentially piggybacking onto another doctor's office routine and staff, while still having the freedom of setting my own schedule and marketing to my own desired patient type. There are many benefits to this arrangement, and oftentimes a decent amount of autonomy. But no, I chose the road less traveled and opted to open my own office in my own empty space. I wanted complete independence, control, and authority over everything about my practice. There would be no one else telling me what hours I would work, no mandatory office meetings to sit in on. On the flip side, there was no marketing girl at the helm (in fact no staff at all) and certainly no patients lined up waiting for me to open my doors. Actually, when I signed the lease for my office there were not even walls yet. There were eight hundred square feet of concrete floors and a to-do list a mile long. I chose this option however, because remember I am a Capricorn and I like to do things *my way*.

Do not misunderstand my situation, I did not have to reinvent the wheel. I hired a well-respected group of consultants to give advice and ideas, at which point I made the final call on every major decision. Anyone familiar with the work and dedication involved in building and managing a successful business knows what I was up against. Not only did I have to design the build-out of my office, I also had the awesome responsibilities of hiring and firing, training and managing employees, inventory and maintenance of products and equipment, the accounting responsibilities of insurance billing, paychecks and taxes, along with the very necessary marketing for patients and referrals. All this plus the skills and stamina necessary to perform accurate and precise chiropractic adjustments was on my radar each and every day. And I loved it. For a little while.

In the beginning, I seemed to thrive on doing it all. My boys were only five-months-old when I opened my doors and the necessary preparation for Hellenbrand Family Chiropractic helped get me through the long days of nursing, bathing, and diapering those little guys. From the time I was old enough to dream about what I wanted to be when I grew up, I envisioned myself forever having a fast-paced, demanding and successful career. I was simply too driven to do anything less. From the feedback I received from my patients, employees, and colleagues, I was doing exactly that. My dream of success was coming true.

Building, owning, and running Hellenbrand Family Chiropractic initially solidified the notion that no challenge was out of reach. When I was younger, this internal drive led me to other successes such as honor roll in High School or passing Organic Chemistry in college. Notice how adept I was even then, at recalibrating my goals to meet the challenge. Passing, *just passing* Organic Chemistry was enough. Taking on challenges simply because someone said I couldn't do it was another source of pride for me. I once took a step aerobics class in college just to prove to a friend that even this uncoordinated person could pass the class. With that same determination and pride, I also enjoyed surpassing my own *self-imposed* limitations. Early in life I had decided that I would never be a runner. I had no desire to be one of those parents running while my child rode his bike alongside me. I had no desire to wear too-short shorts, and definitely did not want to beat my knees into a bloody pulp. Physically speaking, running was akin to a climb up Mt. Everest in that it never made it on my list of necessary accomplishments. I was not physically fluffy, but I was not lean and mean either. This is where I must send a big salute to Mr. Kopf, my high school gym teacher. When he was asking me why I appeared to be so uninterested in running the twelve minute mile…and why I was so melodramatic about my inability to *ever* be a runner, I explained that neither of my parents were athletic and therefore what hope did I really have? He looked at me sternly with his beady little eyes and told me that *I* decide what abilities I possess not the genetics of my parents. I am proud to share with you that only a few short years later I ran my first 5K and lived to tell the tale. You would have thought I had run a marathon with the scrapbook page I made to commemorate the event.

In life we are presented with many such obstacles, and thankfully, we encounter many souls that choose to pick us up and push us forward. Mr. Kopf, to this day, has no idea he was my personal life coach. I have had several people in my lifetime that seemed to present themselves to me at opportune moments and ultimately change the course of my life. Unfortunately, there are also those people we meet that seem to knock us right off our feet and maybe even kick us when we are down. I vividly remember being about twelve years old (in the 1980's when exercising to stay fit was thought to be just another fad) watching Jane Fonda fitness videos in my living room. In my mind, and many others I suspect, she epitomized what every woman wanted to look like. After watching one of those videos I turned to my mother and proudly exclaimed that one day I was going to look just like Jane Fonda. My mother's response? She laughed and said, "I doubt it, Honey." Now, in retrospect, I recognize that she did not intend to stomp on my self-esteem and throw it out the window that day. However, her statement struck a chord with an already struggling tween self image. I swore to myself, in the privacy of my bedroom that night that I was up for the challenge. Twenty-four years later, the success of that personal challenge is still up for debate, but Mr. Kopf gave me the power to make my own decision on the matter.

So, getting back to that chiropractic office of mine…it was January 2004 when I opened my doors and began my career as a chiropractor. I worked day and night, both at the office and at home. I gave this mission of mine everything I had. I was the doctor, the office manager, the x-ray tech, the accountant, even the marketing girl. With the most wonderful receptionist at my side, Claire and I made it our goal to be the best office in town. We worked nights, weekends and the hours in between. I knew and loved my patients and in turn, they knew and loved me and mine. Most of my patients knew my babies by name, occasionally getting to see them run and play when Daddy brought them by the office. These patients were beautiful people who I was helping feel better and live better. Ultimately I found it to be very rewarding, if grueling work. I gave them my blood, sweat and tears. Lots and lots of tears.

I could not have predicted the tears. After a long afternoon at work, I would come home and cry because one of my patients was not improving. What else could I do to help them? What was I missing in their care management? I would cry because a new patient told me they did not *believe* in what I did. Hell, I was not practicing a religion for crying out loud! Other days I found myself crying because I felt like I was missing time with my boys. I had arranged my office hours in a way that I only had to be at the office about twenty-five hours each week. What I had not accounted for was how much more there was to do outside of office hours just to keep the place running. So only a year and a half later, I found myself in a curious predicament where I was no longer happy at home or at my office. Please remember, *I am a perfectionist*, so this was devastating for me. Looking in the mirror each day I fell short of Best Mother *and* Best Doctor, and therefore I felt like I was a failure at both.

I know now that in reality I was doing both jobs damn well. What I did not realize then was that I was giving so much of myself to everyone else, that I had nothing left to give *me* at the end of the day. Sound familiar? In hindsight I now recognize that this hard working, dedicated, control-freak of a woman needed some time to unwind and have no responsibilities at all. I needed a reprioritizing of my life – stat. I hired a life coach to help me better understand the different areas in my life that needed nurturing. I planned an evening away from home one night each week to peruse bookstores, frequent Starbucks, or meet a friend for dinner. I dove back into reading novels where I found a sort of escape from the turmoil in my own life. I even bartered adjustments for private yoga sessions while the babies napped. In the end I was fairly successful at instituting new rituals that were supposed to help me feel more balanced. Of course, the ultimate result of all of that soul searching was my decision to sell the office and be a full-time mom. Prior to that realization however, in the thick of self-improvement manuals and positive affirmations, I looked around and discovered another very important person that was not receiving a fair share of my resources, skills, and love: my husband.

The man that I promised to love, cherish, and honor until the day that I die, the man that supported me through professional school, national boards, and even the financial risk we were taking with my business venture, was not receiving his fair share of love and attention.

While he was holding up his half of the bargain by holding me at night when I was in tears, waking in the middle of night to help care for our little boys, and generally being the best husband and daddy that I could have asked for, I was slacking. Not intentionally, of course. I did not even notice at first. When I sold my office and decided to raise these crazy kids of mine, Brandon was someone that I took for granted and assumed would always be there for me. He put food on the table and a roof over my head. He was someone I snuggled up with at the end of the day and someone always willing to warm my feet in the dead of winter. He patiently loved me and I soaked it up.

A little more background on Brandon might be appropriate at this point. He is one of six children from a devout Catholic family in south central Wisconsin. He is the second-to-youngest child. Brandon was raised on a farm for a good portion of his youth, his father busy in the fields while his mother was doing her best to supplement their income while concomitantly raising six kids. His older siblings were busy being teenagers and since he only had one younger sister he commonly found himself playing alone and rarely found it necessary to engage in a lot of chatter. I tell you this about my husband because he is one of those men whom I have discovered to be emotionally complex *inside*, but who rarely share their feelings on the *outside*. There are positives and negatives to that, of course. It might mean that I am saved from an earsplitting rhetoric on what inappropriate or hurtful thing I just said, but it also means that when I am craving some heartfelt dialogue about a particular topic or event, I rarely get it. Having said that, I found myself one evening having a discussion with my husband about heaven.

We had already retired to our bedroom, the kids tucked safely in their beds. Most nights he crawls into bed, sprawls himself spread eagle, his forearm held tightly over his eyes to shut out the lamplight. (I like to unwind with a good book at night.) Tonight however, we are curled up together, faces close, noses almost touching. We are re-capping our day when I bring up a magazine article I read about heaven. It was actually a collection of essays dedicated to answering frequently asked questions about heaven, giving some of the thoughts and interpretations of four popular Christian writers. And it was fascinating. Let me just say that I firmly believe there is a heaven, and I believe in angels that guide and protect us. In fact, I can tell you the exact moment in my life when *my* guardian angel did just that. Picture a busy four-lane highway at lunchtime rush hour. I was a student at the

University of Wisconsin – Madison, leaving a final exam. The sidewalks which were usually full to the brim with students and bikes were empty that afternoon, I had finished my exam early. I stepped off the curb to cross the street and before I could take my next breath, I was unceremoniously hauled out of the road by a yank of my backpack. I felt, more than saw, the car whiz by my face. When I turned around to thank the person that grabbed me, I found no one. No one within fifty feet of me. I was twenty-two years old. In my mind, there is no other explanation for what happened. My guardian angel decided I had more living to do.

Now, I have read some of the accounts of heaven from people that have "seen the white light" or been given glimpses of the afterlife and survived to share it. I wanted to know what Brandon thought on some of the questions that I always wanted answers to. Does a child continue to grow and age in heaven, or do they stay a child forever? Will I see my dog Oakley in heaven? Are pets even allowed? And the question that stuck with me that day was:

If I die and Brandon remarries, whom would he see in heaven
after his own death?

I can only imagine what the poor guy was thinking as I dumped *this one* on him! Nothing like some brain numbing chitchat to lull us off to sleep, huh?! No, instead his little wifey wants to know if he would have to choose between me and wife #2 on those golden streets. Or would we have to *share him* like Mormons? And when he did die, would he get to choose which lovely wife he visits first? Bless his heart, as uncomfortable as it might have been for him, my silent hero talked with me. *About all of it.* Realistically, we probably did not talk for more than twenty minutes but it was such a profound and insightful conversation that it felt like we spoke for hours.

I have a tendency to be fatalistic (another common trait for Capricorns, it turns out). I admit to worrying when Brandon is late coming home from work, maybe he was in a car accident. Or if the tire swing is spun too fast, I am capable of envisioning my son flying off and breaking his neck right there in front of me, the audible snap like an echo in my head. Since becoming a mother these worries are more frequent and quite frankly more obnoxious. I have a very real fear of one of us dying young from cancer, drowning, a kidnapping, or even a dangerous weather pattern. Much to the dismay of my ever-optimistic husband, a tornado *watch* means the kids are unceremoniously hauled out of bed to camp in the master bedroom just in case a tornado hits our home in the middle of the night. At least we would all die together, goes the rationale. The countless responsibilities of parenthood coupled with the awesome realization that we are raising *human beings* has shaken me to the core at times. When I turned eighteen years old my father took me skydiving and I jumped out of an airplane by myself. No tandem for me thanks. You could not *pay* me to do it again. I have too much in my life to live for now, and I am no longer fearless.

So when we found ourselves talking about death and heaven, I was both invigorated to be having such an openhearted conversation with him, but also sad to be thinking about the reality of our death. Though death is a certainty, it can instill fear and dread in the best of us. I do not fear death because of fire and brimstone, or judgment for my sins. I fear it because I am certain I will terribly miss these beautiful people I share my life with. I fear it because I wonder who will help my husband raise our children. Mothers and fathers are different from each other, I believe, for a reason. Where he will coach his son to get up and shake-it off, I will embrace and kiss the boo-boo. Where he will wrestle with them in the moments just before bed, I will curl up with them and read a story. Balance is key and with two of us, it can be achieved. With only one of us, the equilibrium is off. Of course, I worry too who will warm my husband at night and put hot meals on the table for him? I am thirty-two years old and would prefer to think I have many more years to enjoy crawling into bed with my husband at the end of the day.

Still, the craziest worry of all, I think, while laying next to my husband with my head nestled on his shoulder, was my need for reassurance that he would take care of *me* should I leave this world early. That if my soul should wander with unresolved worries and loneliness, would I find him one day up there with me? I posed the question about a new wife and a new mother for my children. Though Brandon is a man of few words he has spoken beautifully eloquent words of praise and love to me in our most private of moments. The most beautiful gift he has ever given me, however, the most poignant of words he has ever spoken to me, he said that night. He said, "Honey, when I get to heaven I'll find *you* first."

Well, thank heavens for that.

chapter seven

Daddy, The Amazing

As the mother in the household, we oftentimes get a bad rap. We are the enforcer of all things resembling rules: "No, you may not draw all over yourself with that pen...No, you may not play out in the front yard wearing only your underwear...No, there is not time for a wrestling match before bedtime." Not only are we the Enforcer of Rules, we are also the Boss of Clean. "Please put your shoes in the shoe bucket, your towels on the towel rack, your toys in your toy box, and your dishes in the sink"...you get the picture. Therefore, the result is that even though we are also the boo-boo kisser, ultimate hug machine, and the cheek-stroker at bedtime, we are still the "bad guys" because we are the voice of reason to a bunch of children whom *reason* is as foreign as a life without toys. (Really I am only referring to the male half of my offspring since my girl seems to get it, meaning she will be a classically wonderful mother one day.)

It can be incredibly tough sometimes to witness the fun my children have with their father because it is so different from my own version of fun with them. Their fun is usually louder, faster, and more rambunctious than our version of fun. I do however, enjoy seeing them throw caution to the wind. But if life was fair I would have a chapter in my book entitled, "Mommy, the Amazing" in addition to this one. I'm sure there is material enough for it, I'm sure that my children would be more than happy to share recollections of good times and amazing feats of one Kristi Hellenbrand, Best Mom in the World. Until the inspiration comes to me however, we are going to discuss my lovely husband and his role as father in our home.

Admittedly, Brandon is a pretty fantastic husband and father. I admit that I am quite fortunate to have someone who works all week to support his family, meets us for lunch at Chick-fil-A on occasion, and is just about always home by the six o'clock dinner hour. Although he is not known for his culinary skills or his dishwashing, should I ask for help in either department I never receive arguments or grumblings. I rarely get a verbal affirmative either, but I know I will find him behind the sink or in the refrigerator a few minutes later.

As in most homes, the majority of household chores fall squarely on my shoulders and in all honesty I find that fair. It is simply easier for me to squeeze in some vacuuming between Dora Candy Land and Homework Hour, or maybe even find time for some light dusting while the kids are painting their next masterpieces. There are a few exceptions to the rule however, as we both find particular chores repulsing. Give me dust, give me a dirty sink, hell – give me a dirty toilet, but I absolutely refuse to clean a dirty shower. I am not sure if it has to do with the back-breaking-bent-over position you must assume or if it is the nasty hairball (admittedly, mine, as my husband has no hair) that looks as if we have grown a hamster in our shower when we were not looking. Regardless, I adamantly refuse to clean the shower. So my darling husband cleans it. Probably not as frequently as he should, mind you. But this guarantee of forever being free from cleaning our showers comes with a price: laundry.

Yep, the deal is if he can keep the showers clean, I will wash, dry, and hang or fold his laundry. All of it. Nasty, smelly gym clothes notwithstanding. I consider this a fantastic deal from my vantage point, though there was a time when he assumed *wrongly* that ironing was included in the agreement. I set him straight on that right away, explaining that I have already met my lifetime limit of ironing ten years ago while working at a drycleaners. He glumly accepted. For any of you that were unaware that there is such a thing as a *lifetime limit*, now you know. But I have found this card can only be played once, so do not push your luck girls.

Now, let's head outside to the Lawn and Garden Responsibilities of keeping a home. Mowing, weeding, fertilizing, edging, planting, pruning, and pest control are only a few of the myriad of chores to be completed on any given weekend so as not to piss off your neighbors. Owning a full acre of green space is hot commodity, sure, but who wants their husband to spend half of their weekend cutting the lawn? Not me and definitely not our kids. Come Saturday morning the pressure is on for fun, fun and more fun and watching Daddy push a lawn mower is not fun. Enter the All-Time-Best Father's Day gift: a riding lawnmower. It might very well be the one time in our entire relationship that I genuinely surprised my husband. I bought the John Deere with my own spending money, had it delivered and parked in our garage that morning and watched him almost trip over it that night when he came home from work. It is the best couple grand I have ever spent. It cut his lawn maintenance time in half and makes for a fantastically fun ride for the kids. I know, I know, I have heard the warnings. I know the dangers. But you *have* to see my kids' faces when they are sitting up there on Daddy's lap driving that thing. Now, I admit that hooking up a sled behind it during our Georgia snowfall last year probably would have had Child Protective Services all over us, but thus far we have only experienced fun on that lawn tractor, with some fantastic memories to boot.

So all in all, Brandon and I have a pretty good arrangement for accomplishing all of those tedious household chores. This keeps disagreements to a minimum, both of us having fair expectations of each other, allowing for extra energy to field the curve balls our kids send our way. One way we keep a level head about things is the To-Do List. (Yes, it is capitalized in our home.) If you, like me, live with a pie-graphing-Excel-loving-anal retentive husband like my own, you know that you are already behind if you do not have a to-do list somewhere within sight, *at all times.* Now, I used to consider myself a planner. I am acutely aware of the usefulness of sticky notes so I do not forget things, the problem being that I often have a minimum of twenty sticky notes out there *somewhere*, waiting to be realized. This, my husband has decided, *just won't do.* And so my little book of to-do lists was born.

I will admit that Brandon has a point. It does feel rewarding when, at the end of the day, I can cross out three or even four tasks that I performed to completion. I feel free. Free to throw the rest of the day to the wind and do *anything* I choose. I am free to read that trashy novel, shop for something just for me, or eat a bowl of ice cream. Or maybe I will do all three. A weight is lifted off my shoulders that my massage therapist would normally have to knead out. I am a self-described Achiever, therefore I feel fulfilled when I can say that I have accomplished something each day. What I have come to fear about that To-Do List, however, is sitting down and making *the list.* It is daunting. There are usually no fewer than twenty tasks, errands, or projects that I need to complete in order for my life to keep moving forward. These items might be as mundane as "call Mom," or as detailed as "design, build and sew a dress-up wardrobe for Nana's Barbie dolls." Admittedly, there are many weeks when I am resigned to simply transfer over items from my prior to-do list onto my new and improved to-do list. This is when I feel I have failed the to-do list system. (That wardrobe never did get built.)

I have found, however that these beautifully constructed, though oftentimes tedious lists, do allow me to prioritize my life. (Finding that "Galway girl" song to download onto my mp3 player should not take precedence over my yearly dermatological exam, for example.) Had I not had my list, I might have done it all wrong. Or maybe I would have gotten both of them done in the time it took me to prioritize them on my list. I am still unsure. I can tell you this: I unequivocally love that my *husband* has a To-Do List. It allows me to gently suggest that he needs to hang that potted plant from the ceiling, without having to hound him for weeks to do it. He just jots it down on his list and I know it will eventually get done. Maybe not today, and in all likelihood not tomorrow. However, Brandon loathes transferring items from an old To-Do List to a newly revised one, and so it will get done. You might be tempted to ask if I have free rein to put just anything on his list. No. I am never, *ever,* allowed to put something on that list without checking with him first. If I did that it would become a "Honey-Do List" and that is just not cool.

Now I must confess that I have been blessed with a husband that is very handy around the house. Plumbing leak? Put it on the list. Floorboard pulling away from the wall? Put it on the list. Build the kids a playhouse? Put it on the list. Fix the remote control toy dump truck that the kids broke? Put it on the list. And so goes the amazing feats of one "Daddy can do *anything,* Mama!" kind of father. Most of the time, I love this about Brandon. The toy that I would have given up for loss, he can fix. That saves us from many tears over toys that were played with just a little too roughly or the best-loved ones that simply were loved *too long.* Rudolph never mentioned the Loved Dearly, Just Needs Repair Island of toys. My husband is akin to the worker elf that can bring them back to life. Now, if those toys need a stitch sewn here, or a good washing after a night out in the rain, call on me. In most cases, however, the toys that are on their way to the dump need an engineer's mind to reinstate them to the toy box. New batteries I can do. New wiring? Not so much. Good thing Daddy is an engineer.

And so my children have declared, loudly and with much gusto, there is no feat, no job, and no problem too big for their Daddy. The boys, in particular, think that the sun rises and sets when Daddy does. If the impossibly complex Double Loop Hot wheels Race Track needs to be put back together due to a previous demolition derby event in the boys' room, they call on Daddy. If their stuffed bat toy has stopped echolocating, Daddy will extract said speaker system and re-wire it. And so you can see how this *handiness* really benefits me in more ways than one. There are no expensive contractor invoices for the broken washing machine, and no panic-stricken runs to Toys R Us to replace a dearly adored lovie. Not to mention that the kids are learning some handy fixer-upper skills. No complaints, right? Well…except for that *one day* when it caught up with me. The boys were four years old when an impromptu bike ride around the neighborhood was suggested by one fed-up-with-the-fighting mother. Upon getting on their bikes, Tristan advised me that his tires "probably just needed a little more air." On that particular day, at that particular hour, I felt it just was not very necessary to add a few extra PSIs to the tires. They were rideable. Ride kid, ride. That did not fly with them however, so I made the excuse that I could not remember how to do it and couldn't we just get going already? At which point, they declared, clear and proud, "Don't worry Mom! *We* know how to blow up our bike tires even if *you* don't!*" That was the day that I received my very first how-to lesson from my boys. Admittedly, I was impressed that they did in fact know where Daddy kept the air compressor and where he plugs it in and how to put it on the wheel and lock it down. I was impressed. Resulting score? Two points for the kids. Wow. I on the other hand lost one point for lying to them, but gained one for slowing down my harried life long enough for them to demonstrate their skills. So I break even that day. Not all together a bad day.

As a mother, it can be exhausting to hear yet another exclamation of how fast this Hot Wheels car drives compared to that one, or how this doll likes to drink milk, but this one likes orange juice. Or to remember that this red dress is not one that Brooklynn's doll likes to wear, but this pink one is necessary for every Wednesday. Just yesterday, Blake announced that a much venerated stuffed animal is having a birthday party and therefore life must stop so that we can dig through the attic for a baby toy to wrap up for Stingy the Sting Ray. These young people find such joy from what often feels mundane or just plain silly, and yet I have to remind myself that with every crazy feat they perform, a life skill (like air compression dynamics) is being realized. I have to stop and take notice, and thankfully, when I can no longer joyfully participate, Brandon walks in the door and is more than happy to partake in a stingray's birthday party.

Their helpfulness and eagerness is energizing, and their father deserves a lot of credit for instilling the wow factor in even some of the most mundane household chores. Going into the attic is the same as a rocket trip to the moon for these children. With headlamps on their heads and smiles on their faces, changing the air filter on the furnace is an event to remember. Cleaning the ceiling fans is as exhilarating as standing at the top of the Sears tower for my kids, simply because there is a ladder involved. Oh, and that trip up the ladder inspired the tallest Lego tower this side of the Mississippi. They have not even gotten to see Daddy change the oil in the car yet.

It is fun to sit back and watch the simple pleasures that children can get from the very things that we call *chores.* If we slow down long enough to appreciate the teachable moments, the joyful grins, and the usefulness of the extra set of hands wanting to wash dishes, we truly appreciate the beauty of these little ones growing up and growing strong. Super Daddy still needs to save the day when Mommy can't open a new jar of peanut butter, but Super Tristan and Super Blake will be able to step in to fill his shoes soon enough. Mommy is still the one they go to when they fall and scrape their knee, but Brooklynn knows without a doubt that her Daddy hung the moon. This parenting job is a difficult one and two heads is better than one when it comes to parenting these little kids, no matter how great Daddy is. Two sets of hands to hold them, two sets of feet to chase them and two sets of eyes to watch them and keep them safe seem indispensable. Most important however, is two hearts to love them, to cheer them on and to be their best fans.

chapter eight

dreams of a child

As a parent in the midst of chaotic mornings, messy meal times, and even sassy mouths, I frequently find myself looking for affirmations that I am doing *something* right by my children. I have discovered that it is the rituals within our family, big and small, that tend to bring into stark relief just how many wonderful moments there are in my home. For example, it is a tradition in our household that I greet the kids in the morning with a good, long hug. I revel in the ability to still be able to pick them up and feel their heads resting on my shoulder, with their legs wrapped around me just so. I play with their bed head and smell that warm and salty scent of a child just woken. Yeast bread with a dash of salt on it, I think. I inhale deeply, enjoying this slow start to the day, and quietly drop the most vital of questions, "So... what did you dream about?"

Now, nine times out of ten I can tell you exactly what they are going to say. Brooklynn? Three pink, fluffy kitties. Tristan? A great white shark biting a bad man in a boat. Blake? A monster truck that is so big it can jump over a skyscraper. On the rare chance that these are not their answers, they tell me they have dreamt about *me*. At that very moment my heart actually leaps out of my chest, but I pull it together and realize that I have just fallen in love with them all over again. And it is not even seven a.m. yet.

Writing this, I think how wonderful it must be to be so young and find reasons to dream about your favorite things each night. Now, I do appreciate the fact that in all likelihood they have not in fact dreamt about any one of these things probably more than once. But that is what makes it so sweet. They *want* to have dreamt about it, and therefore they did. It's equivalent to an adult starting their day with positive affirmations, or prayer. They are sending the universe a message that they are happy and content and comfortable in their own skin. They are surrounding themselves with comfort in the same way I throw on the same warm sweater each morning when I crawl out of bed. As their mother, when I hear that their dreams have been gentle and precious I rest easy that their souls are worry-free and joyful.

Much has been written about the significance of dreams, some believing they are a looking glass into our innermost being, others thinking dreams tell us about the health of our external shell. Are our dreams a message from God or are they, as the Chinese believe, a separate world that our souls inhabit while our bodies are tied down to this world? I do not have the answer. I can say however, that when my children wake and share with me their pink, fluffy dream players or their most beloved animals or interests having consumed them the night before, *I need not worry*. All is right in the world.

Let's face it: Moms worry. We worry about whether our children are built of strong moral character, and if they have strong enough legs and lungs to keep up with the rest of the kids at school. We worry if they are eating the right foods, washing the germs off their hands, and even holding on tight enough to that tire swing they are riding. If they are coughing we are worried it is pneumonia, if they are cold we are worried it is frostbite. This worrying is part and parcel with motherhood, I think. My husband has referred to me as a "mother hen" when I insist we pluck them from their beds in the middle of a late night tornado watch to keep them close to us. When they were babies this mothering resulted in gentle touches on their foreheads, biceps and chests to check that they are breathing and not feverish before I myself can retire to bed. It is why they wear sweaters when *I* am cold and why we commonly find ourselves with one or more children camping out on our bedroom floor in their sleeping bags. Having acknowledged all of this worrying though, I can honestly say that on those gorgeous mornings when I am holding them in my arms, wrapped in their still sleep-warmed legs and feeling their preciously warm breath on my neck, I know that they feel loved. They feel safe. There are no worries.

Now there have been plenty of mornings when I could have let them in on my little secret. You know…the secret about what they *actually* dreamt about. I have woken on several occasions in the wee hours of the night to hear one of them fussing quietly or whining over the monitor about how their brother stole his favorite toy and would not give it back. Or to Brooklynn whimpering about her Nemo toy having disappeared. Sometimes she chatters in her sleep about her mommy dolls taking care of her baby dolls. Yet still, inevitably that next morning, it is always pink, fluffy kitties that she remembers. Three of them.

I wish I could remember what *I* used to dream about when I was a child. They were probably silly, little mundane things that my universe just happened to revolve around. Maybe it was my Baby Beth doll, or my Western Barbie. Or maybe it was Bo Duke whom I used to kiss before I jumped into bed each night. Yeah...The Dukes of Hazzard was an obsession of mine when I was four and five years old. I had a poster of them with the General Lee car on my wall, and I vividly remember having to crawl up on a chair in order to give Bo a kiss before bed. (Quickly before my parents came into the room to tuck us in, I might add.) I do remember one dream that was a reoccurring theme when I was six or seven years old, and it was quite scary. I have not had it in almost thirty years, but I can remember the experience of it as if it happened last night. It always happened late into the night, and it usually began as pressure in my chest, and an incredible feeling of exhaustion. In my dream I was running, as fast as I could - and I was terrified. Something was chasing me, but to this day I do not know what it was. The fear was not only *what* pursued me, but also *where* I was being chased. Picture a skyscraper with a huge atrium cut out of the middle. Where a railing should have been, to keep people safely on the walkway, there was none. It was a four foot wide hallway that I was running around again and again, with the risk of falling off the edge and down into the pit of the building. So I had to run fast, and I had to run accurately. I never actually fell. I assume that the heavy beating of my heart and rushing feeling I felt in my head is what woke me. I would wake covered in sweat certain that I was about to die. I would manage somehow to get to my parent's room across the hall, but I do not know how exactly. I felt zombie-like, floating there rather than walking, as if I had just rode a conveyer belt to get there. I stood next to the bed motionless, but for a pitiful little "Dad" that squeaked out of my throat. When my dad would rouse enough to ask me what was wrong, I remember trying to explain my bad dream, but feeling unable to do so. Nothing I could say, no words, could describe the horrible feeling of fear and exhaustion I was feeling. Sometimes I felt nauseous, but mostly I just felt overwhelmed and alone. When he scooted over in the bed and invited me in with him, suddenly I could move again and I snuggled into his arms, trying to hide under the covers. Using a soothing voice and a light touch above and around my ear, he would try to talk me down. I am sure he felt my heart pounding against my chest like it wanted to get out. I remember him commenting on it to my mother. He felt my sweat and my jitters and did not understand it other than to try to calm me. And inevitably I would settle back into a sleep, fitful or not, I cannot say. This entire scenario happened maybe three or four times, and I remember my dad being concerned about it, asking me about what might be going on at school or at the babysitters, hoping to find some trigger for the episodes. I do not think we ever discovered what it was, and the dreams did pass with time. The closest thing I have ever experienced to that feeling, in my adult life, was what I call my "panic attack." A one-time event near to the time I sold my office, where I felt like I had a boulder sitting on my chest with the concomitant feeling of being unable to participate with the real world. It lasted for an hour at most and has never come back, thank goodness.

Nowadays my dreams are a variable collection of memories, pleasantries, to-do lists, desires and escapades into my novels, and yes, still on occasions, fears. According to my husband, I tend to mumble in my sleep, usually incoherently, occasionally quite lucidly. If he has eavesdropped on my Outlander novel heartthrob, Jamie Fraser dreams, thankfully, he has never commented. I apparently have busted out a gut laugh in the middle of the night, and then fallen right back into a deep slumber. I wish I could remember *those* dreams since there are not many things that get me laughing that hard.

In the end, I think my husband would rather be woken by my laughter than my sobs, however. And goodness knows, he has been jarred awake by my tears enough in the past fifteen years. There is a common theme to these dreams, usually of loss. Occasionally my deceased grandfather shows up in those dreams. Although we were not all that close when he was alive, (geographically speaking I rarely saw him but for holidays), he made an impression on me. My grandparents rarely came to visit, much to the dismay of my mother, but when I did see Grandpa he had a way of making me feel very special. He loved to garden, and took great pride in his blueberry bushes and bleeding hearts. We used to pick blueberries until my fingers were black from the juices. I admit that I ate more of the blueberries than I actually put in the bucket he gave me but he never once scolded me, and usually sent me home with more. When I got older, he became a coach of sorts. He was the principal of the local high school and for years he encouraged me to do dramatic readings, the debate club, and even coached me on some early writings that I did for school newspapers. It was not that I was particularly good at any one of those things, he just felt that I was *in the process* of being very good at *something*. He was convinced I would do something great with my life and always pushed the ideals of hard work and determination. I learned years later that I have no biological or genetic link to this man, as he adopted my father when Dad was quite young. And still, I felt a connection with him. When I was pre-med in college he was thrilled. When I switched to chiropractic, he said that he was very impressed with the chiropractor in his town and felt I had chosen wisely. When he came down with a terrible disease called Myasthenia Gravis, he called me to get my "expert medical opinion." And when he died of a sudden heart attack only a few years later, I was devastated. I have a blueberry bush in my backyard, in honor of him. When my children eat blueberries until *their* fingers are black, I think of him. And he still pops into my dreams on occasion. Happy tears, sad tears, I have shed both for him in those dreams.

I have not had many losses in my life. My grandfather was the first person in my immediate family to die and I was twenty-three years old when he passed away. Up until then, the losses I had experienced were things like my hamster drowning in the sump pump, or having to send my new kitten to another home because my body decided it could not breathe when he was around. Leaving a best friend behind when our family moved to a new town was also a difficult transition for me when I was young.

My first real loss did not occur until I was a teenager. I was fifteen when my parents divorced. Without going into too many horrible details, my mother chose to leave us for a man whom she had met at work. And it felt as though the world I knew had caved in on itself. For the past seventeen years of my life most of my dream weeping has been associated with that loss, resembling aftershocks or tremors from a persistent earthquake. Sometimes I wake up scared for my father, now living alone in Montana, with no one to take care of him. Now mind you, he is sixty years old and plenty able to take care of himself. But still, I worry about him all the time. I do not worry about him getting sick, though he suffered his first heart attack a few years ago living out there on his own. I do not worry about him driving down those remote highways at night with deer just waiting to jump out in front of him, even though he did hit one once. No. What I worry the most about is if he is *lonely*. Because I remember hearing him cry at night, after my mom left. I remember wanting to console him, but having no idea how. Having no idea what to say to him. No idea if he would prefer that I *not know* he was crying. And so my dreams about my dad now are usually of *him* losing something, or me losing him. I cannot imagine life without him. It is as simple as that.

As you can imagine, the dreams I have of my mother are different from those of my father. I used to dream angry dreams about her and the choices she made in her life. I would wake crying, but filled with rage. I would be shaking with fury and anxiety and be up the rest of the night wondering what had gone wrong in our lives. When I became a mother a few years ago, those dreams dulled and became more and more infrequent. In fact, up until last night I could have said that it had been months, maybe years, since waking up crying about a dream I had starring my mother as the main character. The dream last night opened with my dad, sister and I walking down the aisles of one of those huge supermarkets that we used to shop at when I was a child. Woodman's, I think it was. We were just floating down the aisles, throwing things into the shopping cart, talking and getting along nicely, like a regular Saturday afternoon growing up. We found ourselves checking out at the register and while my dad was paying I looked over and saw my mom in another aisle farther down. She was buying candy and it looked like she was headed to a movie. I walked over and said, "Hi." I gave her a hug as if I had not seen her in a while and missed her. I could smell the musk of her perfume and I could feel her blue sweater soft on my cheek. She told me that she was headed to the movie theater for the afternoon and would I like to join her? My initial reaction was "Yes, sounds great." But then I stopped and looked back at my dad and my sister and realized that I had to choose. I could stay with them…or going with her. I woke up sobbing into my pillow. It brings me to tears even now, writing it down.

I do suspect that our dreams are a sort of window into our insecurities and fears, dreams and wishes. Most of us spend minutes, sometimes hours each day obsessing about these things anyway. I wonder why our hearts cannot rest at night when our eyes do. Why can I not choose the dream I dream tonight? If I could, I would choose the dreams of a child. I want to dream about unicorns. Pink ones, with purple flowing manes. And I want to ride them. Far, far away from the dreams that are trying to catch me and toss me into the closest tissue box. I suspect my father, being a parent himself, would also prefer I dream of unicorns instead of loss and grief and heartache. Maybe even my mother as well. These dreams are like our own soul's hauntings. Our longings, our oftentimes unrealized anxieties. They keep us up at night and drive our thoughts and actions by day. Even if we do not want them to.

So I listen. I listen at night to my children's breathing, their sighs of contentment and their whines of discontent. I go to them if a stroke on their cheek might calm them and I whisper my unconditional love into their ears when they do not know that I am there. You might say that I am haunting them. Walking through their rooms at night to touch the smalls of their backs, tucking them safer into the middle of their beds away from the edge where they might slip and fall out, placing the tips of my fingers in their warm little palms as only best friends do. It is a small gift I can give them as their mother. Sweet dreams my babies, sweet dreams.

chapter nine

seventy-seven weeks

Wise, timeless passages inform us that life is a voyage and we should pause and reflect at each turn of this ever-important expedition we are on. Writing this book is in many ways *my* exercise in pausing, living deliberately and enjoying the journey. Store bookshelves are full of self-help books to guide us through our more stressful moments to find that peace we all yearn for. I have read some of Dale Carnegie's books, a success writer that preaches to stop worrying about tomorrow and start living today. I find myself intrigued by such a notion. I have read many other authors' books that suggest I can simply close my eyes, take a deep breath and exhale my worries while inhaling my dreams. My problems are only problems if I *let* them be problems, right? Or maybe these problems are opportunities in disguise. Maybe I need to join a yoga class, or pause to listen to the Georgia blue jays chirping in the trees on this crisp March morning. I need to slow down and sip and savor each drink of my coffee instead of mindlessly chugging it down. Because I do very much crave what is promised to result from this slowing down. Apparently there is a calmness out there that I have not been privy to in quite some time. Maybe it looks something like a Caribbean sail through the Virgin Islands, or quite possibly it is as simple as the quiet moments before mass begins each Sunday. It all sounds wonderfully blissful. Here is the thing: I have kids.

Not only do I *have* kids, I have kids that still pee all over themselves and they do not seem to care one iota, Yoda. Any mother that has had the chore of accomplishing the basic task in civilization known as *potty training*, knows how heinous an ideal of yoga-esque mornings full of nature listening and introspective-coffee-sipping really is. The sad truth is that in the throws of *this* voyage, we are lucky to get a shower let alone a yoga session, and the sounds of nature we encounter are the sounds of our own children screaming like monkeys. Show me one mother (not consuming mega-doses of Prozac) who enjoys her travels on the Potty Training Super Highway. I dare you.

In the past few years of babyhood, toddlerhood and something I call "twinhood," I have learned a few things. These are in no way new truths or epiphanies as some people are actually born knowing these things and are hardwired to love these realities of life. I am not one of them. So here they are, in no particular order:

#1: Expect the unexpected. (I however, prefer to *plan*.)

#2: Go with the flow. (I prefer to have my *own opinion*.)

#3: Set your sights within reach. (I prefer to WOW myself.)

So the task of potty training tested me, because only *after* this necessary travel through the previously uncharted territory of potty training with each unique little child, does the appreciation for the hard work and patience you mustered up greet you like a welcome flag at the top of Potty Training Mountain. You will be gasping with relief and holding onto that flag like it is a life raft in a hurricane. Only then will there be time for a congratulatory pause to recognize that the axiom *"This too shall pass"* stands tried-and-true. Please note: I am still reaching for that darn flag. I had a hold of it, once. Well maybe twice. The winds blow fierce up here.

I am not going to go into the proper mechanics and/or rules of engagement involved with potty training. In fact, other than references to bowel movements, there will be no pee-pee, tee-tee, wee-wee or poo-poo talk. So rest easy, and yes, if you are reading and eating at the same time, you may proceed. There are plenty of books out there that purport to be the answer for painless potty training. I read them all. I read them twice in fact. I read them when my children were infants and someone suggested I forgo diapers altogether, like our African or Asian ancestors did, simply waiting for the signal when your baby needs to eliminate. I was instructed to simply hold my baby at arms length until they had finished voiding. I have decided that is more complicated now that we eat in restaurants, drive in cars, and generally have clean floors that we want to maintain. When my husband pulled me aside to inform me that we were consuming 12 diapers per day (or 360 per month) for a total cost of one gazillion dollars, in order to keep our infant twin boys happily clean and dry, I read those books all over again. To encourage me further, he offered a running list of at least half a dozen *other things* we could do with that money, including exotic vacations with a paid nanny in tow. Tempting...so I just kept reading, hoping for inspiration previously undiscovered. Then I got pregnant with baby number three.

Though joyously celebrated, baby number three had not been on our to-do list for any time in the near future. Our twin boys were not even two years old when the pregnancy test (conducted secretly one afternoon while Brandon was at the office) confirmed the reason for my general ill feeling every day. So began the next nine months of intense baby making that resulted in my third child, Brooklynn. And so began the cleansing process of throwing those potty training books out the window because just looking at the words poop, pee, elimination, and void made me nauseous. The preposterous idea of standing over a toilet while happily singing potty songs to my twin boys was most definitely out of the question. I was back in survival mode.

Through the past few years I have had an epiphany of sorts, a revelation about children in general: *We do not "train" them.* We can show them, we can encourage them, and if we are horribly ridiculous we can "break them" to follow our lead. I have witnessed a parent breaking their child much like a horse handler breaks a wild horse. It is not pretty. I suspect the long-term consequences of such actions are not much to look at either. I believe potty training is no different than when they are two years old, and insist on dressing themselves. Or when they are four years old and do not want to hold our hand. Later they will tell us they would rather not eat at all, than eat what is on the dinner table. As teenagers they will turn away from us and walk into what we know to be sure mistakes. They want their life to be *on their terms* even if it is as simple as sitting on a potty when they want to. If we stop being so bossy and instead follow their lead, life will be more joyful for everyone involved. We are giving them some freedom to establish their independence, thereby sowing the early seeds of self-esteem while simultaneously keeping our blood pressure within normal limits. Of course, we must still demand respect from them, maintaining the necessary pecking order for a successful family unit to thrive. However, the oftentimes too common and unspoken mantra of Parents Rule and Kids Drool is simply disrespectful to our little people and hard to maintain without driving a chasm between them and us. Applied to the awesome task of potty training, the lesson I learned – the hard way, mind you – was to let them potty train when *they* are ready. In my case, When They Were Ready did not jive with my four-month prego body and I missed the boat. It set sail without me on it and it did not come back looking for me for a good long while.

I still remember the exact moment I should have jumped on that dang boat. Our family was on vacation in Panama City Beach. I was pregnant with Brooklynn at the time, grossly nauseous all day long, and cranky to boot. Of course, this is when my son Tristan decided that he wanted to sit on the potty and be a big boy. We were in the bathroom, pulling down a dirty pull-up when Tristan said, "Mama, I sit on potty???" Do you know what my response was? I said, "No way, kiddo." At which point my father-in-law's jaw dropped open and slammed onto the floor. When he was able to pick it back up again, he said, "Wow, your kid wants to potty train and you say, no?" With every bone of my body feeling certain I had every right in the world to do so and a mind clear enough to make such a decision, I simply stated, "That's right, Richard. We'll do it when I feel better."

Fast forward almost eight months and I came to the full realization of what I did that day. I would come to regret that one little moment more than I can express in words. It took me *seventy-seven* weeks to potty train my boys because I wanted them to do it when *I* wanted them to do it. I am known for being stubborn and therefore have had the unfortunate gift of having learned many of life's lessons the hard way. Anyone who knows me well can attest to that. But I am coming around and I have realized that I can apply what I have learned in those seventy-seven weeks to other parenting obstacles. My boys were walking by ten months old, and running and screaming simultaneously, soon thereafter. My little girl, on the other hand, decided she wanted to test her mother's panic button and my self-diagnosed disease I have come to call "Doctor Syndrome" and not walk until she was eighteen-months-old. Doctor Syndrome is something that begins to happen when you are studying medicine or nursing or even chiropractic, where you become acutely aware of everything that can go wrong, no matter how rare or unusual it might be. It means that when your child is eight-months-old with their first runny nose you are convinced they have pneumonia. And when they fall off their bike for the first time you are checking their mastoid bone for bruising and expecting cerebrospinal fluid to be dripping out of their nose indicating a skull fracture that might just go undiagnosed. Some of this concern is just part and parcel to motherhood, some of it is paranoia from reading What to Expect When you are Expecting (which in my opinion should be titled All the Things That Can and

Will Go Wrong With Your Pregnancy and Child). What I learned from the pediatric orthopedist that examined Brooklynn at seventeen-months-old, was both a slap in my face and a great relief. He did a thorough examination, asked a book's worth of questions and diagnosed, "She's just at the bottom of the bell curve. Some children have to be at the bottom or it wouldn't be a bell curve." Got it, Doc. Thank you. Even if he did just tell me what I innately already knew, the visit was worth every penny. A month after that appointment Brooklynn decided to walk. She decided, not me. My job was simply to let her do it on her own timeline and clap profusely when she did.

Another example of my children teaching me how to parent happened a few years earlier when my almost-two-year-old Tristan was still refusing to speak even one word from that pretty little mouth of his. While his twin brother was like an Energizer Bunny that just kept talking and talking, my little Tristan was mute. Regardless of his lack of speech, Tristan was the leader of the two boys and quickly became the one labeled, "Trouble" in their "Double Trouble" nicknames so proudly given to them by their father. It did not matter that Tristan could not verbally ask Blake to join him in the fun, he just looked at him a certain way, or maybe there were unseen chemical airwaves of "pecking order" floating through the air, but it was established very early on that whatever he could dream up, Blake must follow. That was when we finally came to the realization that Tristan was not talking because *he did not need to talk.* Blake did it for him. We did it for him. We heard him anyway. Needless to say, Tristan did eventually begin verbalizing and when he did he never babbled or stuttered, but progressed quickly to sentences and beyond. He too, taught me to stop worrying and to honor that each of us have our strengths and weaknesses and are developing on our own God-given timeline. Brooklynn is a born thumb-sucker and now rather than sweating it, I rest assured knowing that there are very few twenty-year-olds out there that still suck their thumb. Her day will come. We all have our day for each new challenge to be met and won.

FYI: Brooklynn potty trained herself in just *two weeks.*

chapter ten

today is a good day for marshmallows

I am having one of those insanely difficult mornings when I cannot decide whether I should take my kids out of the house for the sake of my sanity, or keep them home to teach them a lesson. Their bad behavior this morning (to include biting, spitting, throwing and yelling – and it is only 9:30am) is supposed to mean there will be no play dates later. That is the rule anyway. That is also the *problem*. These are the exact sort of days when I most need to escape the confines of our home. It is not so much that I am not used to these occasional bad days, and the kids did not wake up today consciously deciding to be defiant and ornery. In fact, they were really quite pleasant upon waking. It is Tuesday and in my home that means there is no school today. There is no quick inhalation of breakfast and running out the door before the sun is up. Instead they get to crawl into bed with Mama for a nice, warm "dog pile" to greet the day. It means cartoons and maybe even a pancake picnic on the floor, with frozen blueberries on the side. *This is heaven for us.* All is going well, beautifully in fact, until about nine o'clock. At the magic hour of nine, Tristan and Blake decide that being good little boys is just way too boring and that acting like animals is more up their alley. Now, hush, hush all of you child psychologists. I am fully aware that the decision was not made with as much thought process as I just described. I also recognize that children are never really *out to get you.* I just happened to get caught in the train wreck today and I am feeling a little sorry for myself.

God bless them, I honestly believe that children are programmed to wake each day expecting to have their best day *ever,* and should things not go as planned they might raise a little cane. Maybe their agenda for the day included turning the living room into a swimming pool and I got in the way. Or maybe they had planned on dressing down to their undies and running around singing "shake, shake, shake my butt," while arguing about who is shaking better and longer. I am fortunate enough to have survived both of these scenarios in the recent months and therefore really would not have been too surprised or upset by either. I suppose they are breaking me in, desensitizing me to their boyish antics so that one day nothing with surprise me. However, today, not being privy to their unspoken agenda, I blew it. I was so pleased with how the morning was going, they were so polite at breakfast, even helping me clean up the breakfast dishes and helping their sister to the potty. I was so sure my boys were going to be wonderful little epitomes of good behavior that I had even been contemplating a grocery run to Wal-Mart with all three kids in tow. Not. So. Fast.

Sometimes I think that if I was a good mother I would always hope for the best, but expect the worse. I would have been ready for the bubble to burst, I would have been *cautiously* enjoying each minute of joy in my day, happy for the hour and a half that I got, and ready with a distraction when the walls would inevitably come crashing down. Here is the problem: I am not bipolar. I am a generally happy person and when I am having a good day, I throw myself into it. Children, on the other hand, are all bipolar. One minute they are crying tears of sadness over an unshared toy and the very next moment they can be laughing hysterically because of some commercial on TV featuring a squirrel. Or maybe they can be so mad that they are actually growling, daggers shooting out of their eyes, but the very next instant they are hugging, loving, and kissing their sibling for no reason whatsoever. If you blink you have missed it.

In contrast with my children, I am not programmed to wake up happy each morning. More often than not, when faced with the screeching alarm clock, I punch the snooze button a few times, enjoy some long and exaggerated yawns, and eventually equip myself with a steely resolution to *try* to have a good morning. A calm and completely predictable day is usually what I wish for. Maybe a day with no disciplining, no whining, and definitely no complicated meals to prepare would be nice. Quite possibly I am hard-wired like a two-year-old, preferring routine, playtime and a regular schedule of food that I do not have to prepare myself. How beautifully predictable that sounds, right? Now, please do not misunderstand. Spontaneity is fun *once in a while.* I do not feel put-off when my children request a trip to the jumpy house or even a swim at the local pool. No problem. If a girlfriend calls for a coffee date or a trip to the park, I am excited for an outing. On the other hand, an impromptu executive decision by my husband to set up the tent in the backyard (complete with promises of a full-fledged campfire, s'mores and firefly catching) at five o'clock on a Saturday is met with a complete lack of enthusiasm on my part. I simply find it more difficult to participate happily when I do not know what is coming. So lying there in bed each morning I recognize my weaknesses and pray for the fortitude to have a sunny day with the patience and ingenuity my children demand.

Now for some of you, a sunny day is a given. Try as I might, I am not one of those people that are perpetually happy. I wish I could be. I wish I could always have a smile on my face. I wish I could always see the silver lining. Let's make some lemonade, kids! The truth however, is that my emotions can be greatly altered by the company that I keep. If Brandon is sitting at the computer getting stressed out about our budget, then I commonly become grumpy and stressed as well. If Tristan wakes up and decides to antagonize everyone in his path – twice – then I will be irritable within thirty seconds of saying good morning to him. I used to consider myself *steady*. My mood being predictable, I could hold my own. If I was happy, I was happy. If I was pissed, avoid me for the rest of the day, and look me up tomorrow. Steady happy, steady ornery, regardless, I was *steady*.

I have met chronically happy people who exude happiness everywhere they go and with everyone they meet. From what I have read they will live long, healthy lives and I am jealous of them. I have also seen imposters. You know the ones that I mean…they almost look ill with happiness. Their smiles look so tight that if bumped into they would crack into a million pieces right there on the street. I would put money down that they do actually crack in the privacy of their homes. A couple of months ago, I was calling around for a short-term babysitter and I suspect that a prospective hire fell squarely into this category of people. Her ad read like a Mary Poppins resume, brimming with warm fuzzy feelings. When I called her to schedule a time to meet, her tween daughter informed me that her mother was having a bad day and had *locked herself in the bathroom.* She added that I could try calling her on her cell phone if it was an emergency. Warm fuzzies gone.

My desire for calm and happiness has been especially evident to me since having kids. When my boys were mere months old I found a group of mothers at a Mommy-n-Me music class at the local library. We all had similarly aged infants and the same desire for adult conversation. In addition to our weekly singsong get-togethers, we began getting together for play dates to share mommy gripes, mommy unknowns (potty training, etc) and mommy-daddy dramas. For the past four years we continue to get together, albeit irregularly. A few months ago I sat with a small group of them and we were talking about the trials of staying steady midst the chaos of motherhood. In the course of our discussion I was shocked to discover that four of the original eight women in our group were on one form or another of anti-depressants. How disheartening. I immediately wondered if they were all actually depressed or if this was an example of our country's "medicate them" mentality. Are these women happy now, or have they only chemically altered their brain to trick themselves into *thinking* they are happy? Or maybe like my own mother's response to antidepressants, they are just numb to any emotion at all. So many questions ran threw my head. Maybe I needed some of these happy pills. Maybe my children would be better off if Mommy was slightly drunk on happiness every day. This epidemic of depression is frightening. Our children are being diagnosed as depressed and our teens are following a childhood of Ritalin with a teenhood of Prozac. What is the answer?

One of my best friends, Melissa, shared with me a story about a weekend away that she took in order to recharge and escape from the pressures of her life. Her husband is a pilot and he is gone for seven days at a time, so she is essentially a single parent every other week. There are benefits to having a pilot husband, of course. For one, she gets to have him home 24/7 for the eight days he is home. The rest of us have husbands with only three weeks of vacation we get each year. However, Melissa is a traveler by heart. When he is finally home, she feels the urge to take the family on a trip. In contrast, Brad is tired of hotels and restaurant meals and only desires the comforts of home. In so many ways they are perfect for each other, in so many other ways they can drive each other batty. Sounds familiar, right? So recently Melissa decided to take herself, alone, on a trip. Three full days by herself, away from the stresses of children and the responsibilities of home, she spent the whole weekend relaxing and feeling young again. She was calm, back on purpose and recharged when she was driving back. With a smile on her face and a bounce in her step she walked in the door and within *thirty seconds flat* the stress of life came rushing back into her blood stream. (Ironically correlating to the very moment her five-year-old son demanded a five-year-old something.) The benefit of an entire weekend away gone in thirty seconds.

This leads me to wonder if we would better parent our children and better handle our own stresses if we also had bipolar tendencies. Would we roll with the flow better? Or is it possible that a job requirement for motherhood be Prozac so that we are not railroaded at every turn of emotion that our munchkins hurl at us? The human psyche dreams of happiness, it is innate. Few would disagree with that. So how can I better create my own happiness? I am not so ignorant to think that everyone around me is responsible for making me happy. That would be a hefty weight upon the shoulders of everyone in my household. In fact, when my mother suffered the worst from her depression, we all walked on eggshells trying to create happiness in her that was not ours to create. I certainly do not want my children to feel this way. I want them to have the normal stresses of childhood, but not the stresses of their mother.

Observing my children on any given day I am certain that they do not have the recommended amount of St. John's wart in their system to bring about all of this perpetual happiness. I know that they have not had a glass of wine or their daily dose of Prozac to radiate this level of joy. Blake said to me yesterday, out of the blue and with an ear-to-ear smile on his face that "Today is a good day for marshmallows, Mom." Instantly, the entire population of children in my household was off toward one of the best days of their lives. Simply because with a chill in the air, marshmallows are sure to follow, usually floating in hot chocolate. *His* prescription for happiness was simple.

So I have decided to find my own perfect prescription for happiness. Some of my own quick fixes include dark chocolate, red wine or even an entire box of cookies if the mood arises. A walk with one of the dogs, or a run with my mp3 player (depending on the level of escape required) has also worked to cleanse me of the grumpies. At their blissfully young age, so much of my children's life is really all about the simple pleasures. Children want to feel loved, they want to be fed, and they really, *really* want to play. What a simple formula. Even in the worst of conditions, it seems, kids can make lemonade. They can make it *every morning*. They can be greeted by yet another Monday, another day of school, another day of the requirements of brushing their teeth, getting dressed and having to potty themselves. And if their brother upsets them, it is only a matter of minutes before all is forgiven. In the case of Brooklynn, a nice clean pair of Ariel panties will make her day shine even if it's raining outside. I want some of that. Sign me up. In the meantime, Blake is crawling into my lap singing, "I love you all the time." I had better go. *This* is my box of cookies today. These moments are *my* marshmallows.

can I have that sticky note back?

Iam sitting at Starbucks tonight having just left a Women's Faith Formation meeting at my church. It is one of my "mommy nights" when Brandon has gifted me with a night of adult conversation, away from the nightly responsibilities of house and kids. If judged purely by its name, the meeting sounds like a rather stuffy prayer group or Bible study meeting, but in fact it is a book club for women in our parish. The intention of the group I believe is to share good Christian literature, apply our Catholic teachings to the discussion of the book, and lastly, to simply enjoy each other's company. We meet twice a month on Monday evenings and at the moment we are reading <u>The Shack</u>, by William Young, which has proven to be a difficult read for some of the more, shall I say…old-school Catholics. It seems a fantastically fun read for the rest of us, however. The women in our group are all from varying backgrounds, each having their own unique life story, many of whom have a great knowledge of our faith and others who have significantly less. I have never felt out of place with these women, even though I am by far the youngest in the group and probably the most ignorant one when it comes to our chosen faith. What we share in common is that we are all playing the role of mother, daughter, wife, and friend, to varying degrees of course, but we all want to do it to our fullest. This gives me immense pleasure to be in their company.

It so happens that attending this group also follows along nicely with my recent yearning for an authentic life, giving me new perspective while writing this book. On some evenings, in addition to book club discussions and my regular tag-along coffee, there is the added pleasure of fresh baked cookies or heartfelt stories from the ladies, which is always a nice treat. As a rule we usually leave with a warm fuzzy feeling at the end of the evening. Tonight was no exception, but the warm fuzzy feelings were secondary to the stitch in my side from all the laughter. A personal story, straight from my own lips, evoked the silly laughter and loud hoots heard throughout the walls of the church that night. I will come back to that story in a bit.

To stage the storyline, I feel I must first share with you some of my life's journey within the Catholic Church. Stop now if you are waiting for a fire and brimstone moment, a bedside visit by a saint, or heaven forbid a visit from God himself. No. There have been no halos or angel wings seen on my watch. Each day I live on this earth I am coming to realize that when God speaks directly to me He foregoes the loud, booming voice and opts instead for the whisper. He knows I am a poor listener, so He does this in hopes that one day I will *not* be a poor listener, I think. As a young mother, I believe I have heard him whisper a few times in my life. When all three of my children are crying, screaming and fussing in the backseat of the car, and I feel like I am in the process of literally *losing my mind*, God has whispered, "Pray." Silently reciting the Hail Mary repeatedly until the backseat has magically morphed back into something more human, are a few of my more grace-filled mommy moments. The repetition is calming, the words inspiring. "Pray for us sinners" does in fact encompass the sinful feelings of wanting to physically throw my children out on the street at those moments, and rarely do my children not respond with a calmness that no earthly phenomenon can explain. This graceful art takes a tremendous amount of faith and patience, however. Both of which I have been slow to learn.

Growing up in a relatively small Midwestern town, my parents elected to send my sister and me to the Catholic school that sat only a block from our home. The campus was very much like what you would picture a private religious school to be like in the early 1980's: statues of saints adorning the lawn and hallways, nuns serving as our teachers (one of them even became our first female principal, as I recall), days begun with prayer and silent reflection, with the parent church sitting directly across the street for easy transport of students to our mandatory Friday mass. My sister and I happily occupied space there, coming to realize even at a very young age that bullies and bad words reside just as heavily in small Catholic schools as they do anywhere else. Forgiveness was assumed, tolerance was preached, and I believe that life there within their walls was relatively typical of any elementary school. All was well for several years, meaning I have very few recollections of my first few years there. I do, however, vividly remember forth grade as that was the year that I was yanked out of Sister Nancy's classroom so fast she never had a chance to pull the ruler out on me (a vicious rumor, I'm sure, that she even had one.) Sitting in class one spring day, sometime around the noon hour, the lights were dimmed and we were watching a video about raccoons. My best friend Susan points at Sister Nancy sitting at the back of the room, watching her own television program. Susan smiles, hums along with the softly heard music coming from the back of the room, and then in her best TV announcer voice says, "These are the Days of Our Lives." It turns out that the song I kept hearing in the back of my classroom every day around lunch was the theme song to the popular daytime soap opera. Well, Sue happens to mention this silly story to her mother, who calls my mother, who I am sure called the principal right after she cursed the tuition she had been paying. That was the year that my sister and I began our public school education.

Now, recalling that one crazy day in forth grade does nothing to lessen the fond memories I have of my early elementary education. I fondly recall the name of my kindergarten teacher, Mrs. Braun, and still profess to adore her, brown spectacles and yellow teeth be damned. I remember the first time I was chased by a boy. His name was Eddie, we were in first grade, and he was very cute. It so happens however, that when he was chasing me one day I fell down and skinned my knee. From that day on I was not as impressed with him anymore. Eddie will come up in a later chapter of my life, and also in this book. He goes by Ed these days.

While raising my own children, my boys now matriculating into kindergarten, I wonder what they will remember about their early years in school, and why. I find it fascinating that I can remember we were watching a video about raccoons that day in Sister Nancy's forth grade class, but have almost no memory at all about my third grade experience. Why the lapse? While I am busy fielding possible concerns about my sons' teachers this year is it possible that this entire school year will go without notice in their own memory bank? Is it possible that third grade had no bearing whatsoever on my personal development and that this year might be Tristan or Blake's equivalent of a ghost year? After my scandalous private school experience and as-of-yet-not-mentioned lifelong record of shotty church attendance, you might wonder how it is that I am still Catholic, or that God forbid, I am actually paying private Christian school tuition for my own children. There is a simple answer: my religious journey did not end when my knees no longer bent for mass every Friday at school. It is true that while growing up our family did not receive awards for best attendance at our church and my mother would probably concede that we did not go every Sunday but that it was our *goal* to go every

Sunday (and "that is what matters"). In all fairness we probably went to fifty percent of the masses during any given calendar year and I have mixed memories of those Sundays. At their best, those masses were characterized by acute suffering for forty five minutes (with terrible hunger pangs) through the traditional Roman Catholic mass of sit, stand, kneel, sit again, stand again for a very long time, and kneel until your legs are wobbly with impatience and fatigue. The entire mass was spent with only one thing on my mind: the largest, gooiest, butter-laden cinnamon rolls on the planet to be enjoyed after church at O'Malley's Farm Café. The hot chocolate was not bad either. The multitude of physical pains endured through mass all but subsided when we smelled the sweet cinnamon and sugar adrift in the air. To this day I am unsure why my mother had a rule about not eating anything on Sunday morning until after receiving the Eucharist. I am sure that my fellow women at Faith Formation could fill me in on that, but I am a firm believer that taking two crazy hungry, growing girls to church without breakfast is only asking for a nasty bitch session in the backseat. I say this was my "at best" experience of church simply because of those cinnamon rolls. At worst, my parents were having their own bitch session in the front seat which could ultimately result in a detour past O'Malley's and straight home. Bummer.

Over the years, as my parents began to drift apart from each other, our church attendance dwindled to major holidays and maybe Lent. We always observed Christmas and Easter and still were instructed to give up something for Lent. I laugh at some of the things I was giving up as a child: chocolate, candy, my Barbie dolls, my sister (that one did not fly). As an adult Catholic I still give up some of those same simple things but I have come to realize that giving something up is not as important as *doing something I was not doing before.* I still give up coffee or treats but now I take the money I would have spent on them and donate it to charity. I have placed phone calls to family members that I know have been waiting a good long while to hear from me and have written letters to those that have given up on me altogether. I still refrain from meat on Fridays, except when I forget.

One of the few church sponsored holidays that I have fond memories of during my childhood was Good Friday. It was the one time each year that I pulled out my Bible, with no complaints at all, and *read it.* I believe it was The Classic Children's Bible version, given to me by my Uncle Jim at my First Communion, with delightful illustrations and words I could interpret. It was my mother's rule that from twelve o'clock noon until three o'clock in the afternoon on Good Friday there was no TV, radio or outside noise. We were instructed to grab a seat somewhere by ourselves, read our Bible, pray, or otherwise just be quiet. And I did not mind it one bit. That seems strange looking back now, that I did not once rebel against that. And actually, for the first time in probably twenty some years, I observed those three hours with my own family this past Lent. My husband found it all very strange, as I had never told him about my family tradition before, while my four-year-olds treated it as any other quiet time in the house. We did read a couple of age appropriate bible stories to them, but otherwise they were free to roam and play quietly for the afternoon.

The week after Good Friday inherently found my bible being put up somewhere on a tall bookshelf and left to its own devises for approximately three hundred and sixty two days. The only other time I remember pulling out a Bible as a child is the *singular* time I sassed my mother so badly that she made me copy several pages out of it, word for word, punctuation included. If she had really wanted to get me she would have chosen that Bible passage when the entire lineage of Christ is listed, for what seems to be at least a hundred generations. You know the one that I mean? Well, thankfully, she did not choose that page, but some other one that I honestly do not remember. I do remember it took almost ten notebook pages, front and back to copy it all though. Needless to say I never called her *that* name again. At least not to her face. So my childhood experience with the Catholic Church and its teachings is spotty at best, and horrendously inaccurate and painful at worst.

As I grew into a teenager I knew that some of my friends went regularly to church on Sundays, and some even spent a week each summer at a Christian summer camp. I also came to recognize that all of them had a blast there, and none of them were Catholic. Our church did not take an active role in engaging teenagers in the church community and I only understand now, twenty years later, how crucial a step youth ministry is to keep young followers interested in their faith. In contrast, what I personally witnessed was my newly single-parent father struggling to do his best to raise his girls while receiving what I have come to label as "hate mail" from our church. Once a year my father received a letter from our church telling him how much "back-money" he owed the church. Never mind that he was not receiving child support to raise his kids, never mind that he lost the house and was paying rent to keep a roof over our head, never mind that my sister and I had the average demands of any teenage girl for new clothes and shoes and pretty things(!). Once a year, he sat with that letter in his hand and cursed the church for not knowing, not caring, and not getting off his back. And though he cursed quietly, I heard every word of it and I hated how that letter made my father feel.

So fast forward almost twenty years and I now live in a small town in Georgia and am a member of the most fantastic Catholic Church. I could not have dreamed up a better church to be a member of. In fact, we drive a full thirty minutes (past *the other* Catholic Church that is only five minutes from our house) every Sunday to worship and praise our good Lord and his works. Nine times out of ten, we get a good laugh there too, or a good fatherly swatting. Enter our priest, Father Vic. He is in his mid to late thirties, so already he breaks the traditional mold of a Catholic priest, but more than just his youth and vigor, he stands up in front of us each week and delivers engaging and thought provoking sermons. He does not read them from note cards, thank the heavens. He prefers to look you in the eye. He will commonly throw in a humorous tidbit of information that wakes up those that have still managed to dose off or faze out, and has been known to make personal references (though he will deny it) if you happen to fit the bill for a lesson needing to be learned. We are continually chided each week for not moving to the center of the aisles as we filter into the church to encourage a sense of togetherness and family within his walls. If your cell phone rings in the middle of mass, he will nonchalantly ask how someone got to be so important that they are getting a direct phone call from God. If people arrive late to the eleven o'clock mass, he will remark that the 11:10 mass can now begin. He takes his job seriously, but with humor and self-deprecation sprinkled throughout his lessons. How refreshing!

Not only does Father Vic seem to enjoy his priestly duties, but he also enjoys participating in extracurriculars with his parishioners. My husband began playing in a newly formed church basketball league last year. Quite frankly, this is a group of middle age men wishing they were young again, playing their tails off for nothing other than the enjoyment of playing. There are no trophies won, and nine times out of ten, our team trails by twenty or more points at the end of any given game. But it is absolutely incredible to see these guys run and sweat and play their hearts out, just for the pleasure of playing the game. And no one enjoys it more and plays harder than Father Vic. In fact, it is altogether possible that he would have received the award last year for Most Personal Fouls. Yep, our priest probably checked, hip-bumped and shoved more opponents than any other player in the league. That is his charm, I suppose. That, along with his propensity for gym shorts and flip-flops under that priestly robe of his.

So let us get to the point. Has my perspective of Catholicism changed since becoming a member of this church? Certainly no part of the Catholic catechism has been altered and changed to fit the more lively or engaged bunch of Catholics that define my parish. The mass still follows the same order and predictability that it has for the thousands of years it has been conducted. However, I cannot call it mundane any longer. I rarely want to fall asleep during the sermon, though my young children still do. I no longer lay in bed every Sunday wishing that it was any day other than Sunday because then I would not have to go to church. I freely admit that we do have a family tradition of going for yummy muffins and bagels after mass, which help get my children out the door every Sunday, but I do not believe the tummy splurge accounts for the pleasant nature we mostly assume on the way there. Mind you, my children attend mass with fully satiated stomachs, one lesson learned from my own upbringing.

I used to think that being a Catholic now is easier simply because I enjoy going to mass on Sunday, or because I genuinely look forward to the message behind the readings and the sermon. My sister would argue that in fact I *do* have it easier for those very reasons. But I have to consider that being Catholic is not just going to mass on Sundays. The *big stuff* is not any easier. The forgiveness, the unselfish love for our neighbors, the service we are instructed to demonstrate to those around us and for those less fortunate than ourselves. Those things are still just as hard. Praying each day is *still hard.* Following my Lenten promises is *still hard.* I discovered last year however, that even Father Vic thinks Lent is pretty tough. I know this because while volunteering to help clean up and paint the rectory last year, my husband heard Father Vic talking to himself about how great that hot dog looked on the grill and even though he gave up meat for Lent....maybe just one hot dog would be okay. (What?!?!) It turns out even Father Vic fights with himself over issues such as this. Wow.

So we all make mistakes and can find life difficult. That is a really good thing for this particular sinner, and I will tell you why. Picture a special evening mass devoted solely for the sacrament of confession. Four or five guest priests are brought in to accommodate the masses of people that show up twice a year to confess their sins and receive absolution. Imagine me in a line, holding my sticky note with all of the things I would like to confess. Yes, I have already admitted to being one of those Type A people, and I am a Type A sinner as well. I wrote it all down, word for word, I did not want to forget anything. So I am in line, secretly hoping that my line moves quickly, but that I do not wind up standing in front of Father Vic confessing my lowliest of sins. I would prefer a priest that I do not know, from a parish far, far away to hear about my lack of patience and tendency to yell. But God would have it otherwise. There I am, looking at Father Vic...so I begin. "Forgive me Father, for I have sinned...." and one by one I begin reading my list. It is painful, though I suppose it is not supposed to be fun. Then the unimaginable happens. He says, "Give me that," and he grabs my list and begins reading it to himself! *OMG.* "Hmmm....yep, that judging-others-thing has got to stop because your children are hearing you....okay, yeah, have some more patience....Okay, so..." and he quickly moves to place his hand on my head and pray the Prayer of Absolution. At which point, I interrupt him with an apologetic grin and say, "Wait, Father. *There are some more on the back.*" God help me (literally), Father Vic almost laughed! He shook his head, grinned and said, "You're good. It's all good." Then he pocketed my sticky note.

So, to this day I wonder at what point he was doing his laundry and pulled out my double-sided sticky note of all the sins of my heart. And what did he think? Did he shake his head and think I am hopeless and God help my husband and children? Did he grin and laugh? I will never know, of course. I can report that when I shared my sticky note abduction with the women at Faith Formation, they laughed good, hearty laughs. And though I chose to forego a sticky note at my more recent confessions, I do continue to go and ask for forgiveness. Much like I expect my children to apologize for their minor little transgressions (such as teasing, shoving and generally being disagreeable) all in the name of receiving their mother's forgiveness and boundless love. I suspect my God does the same for me.

chapter twelve

thou shall not wake up your baby sister

Okay. There are things that set me off, and then there are things *THAT SET ME OFF*. And how can two little boys, so small, so helpless, so four years old, set me off? *Waking up their little sister*. Is this reasonable? I envision most people patting me on the back saying, "Children will be children, after all." I recognize and often find humorous and quite fun the euphemism "Boys will be boys." They are made of snakes and snails and puppy dog tails, right? Running, laughing, jumping, launching - all performed while simultaneously tackling and screaming - is what boys do. And I love it. *Unless there is a sleeping baby in the house.*

When the boisterous screaming starts, when the couch has become their trampoline, nine times out of ten the baby just happens to be sleeping. As the decibel level increases I begin to create in my head a running list of why they should respect the dozing little bundle of softness in the room down the hall, otherwise known as their baby sister. First, babies need their sleep. They grow when they sleep, and their bodies heal when they sleep. That tiny little pea all wrapped in blankets is busy getting longer, stronger and is in all likelihood fighting invaders of health such as viruses, when she sleeps. Secondly, babies who do not get enough sleep tend to be…shall we say in lieu of a more malignant word, crabby. They cry more, fuss more, and generally make the lives of those around them feel just a tad less pleasant. The ultimate reason however, that I request a quiet naptime is that once a baby wakes up, they will not go back down. If a baby is rudely woken by a raucous game of Hungry Hippos, the road map you were trying to navigate for the greatest amount of ease and joy in your day may as well be thrown out the window. Everyone in the household has just found themselves on an unpaved, gravel road littered with nature-made speed bumps and certain mud and muck. Let us not kid ourselves. It will probably be bedtime before we find civilization again. Each of these explanations has been given to my boys to explain the necessity of the "quiet hour" in our home and of course, my boys do not buy it.

These boys of mine have reasons of their own why it seems so heinous for there to *even exist* something called quiet time. In all truthfulness, their reasons seem quiet valid if offered to other preschoolers rather than to an irate mother standing with her hands on her hips. First, my boys explain, racecars are *supposed* to swap paint when they are racing. Throwing match box cars down the stairs seems to accomplish the paint swapping better than any other method, my wall paint notwithstanding. "Well actually, Mama, *real* trains make a lot of noise," states Blake. So how am I to argue when Thomas the Tank Engine is whooing and dinging and choo-chooing at a decibel level reserved for commercial jet engines? I feel defeated already, and we are only two minutes into quiet time.

Over the years of observing, reacting and attempting to prevent naptime from becoming a NASCAR-worthy event in our house, I have quite by accident come upon my own theory to explain young boys and their endless activity and noise. Mind you, I do not have hard evidence to back this up. There is no scientific data to support my theory unless you count my homegrown laboratory with its ready and willing male members whom have been scrutinized, categorized, and centrifuged. And given the scientific definition of a hypothesis, I am not even sure my theory falls into that testable distinction. This rationalization seems to take the edge off my ever-rising temper however, because it forces me to see and appreciate the transitory nature of life with children. It helps to explain *why* it is what it is. Here is my theory. Drum roll, please:

Every young man is born with an allotted number of words to speak before they will run out.

Picture an hourglass with each grain of sand being one word they will shout, utter, or articulate in their lifetime. During the first, say eight years of life, the hourglass that is their Life's Words is being shaken, spun, and generally thrown all about, like the contents of a blender with its top left off. Words are pouring out like Niagara Falls in a hurricane. This explains the ever-present "Mama, Mama, Mama..." way of trying to get my attention, when we all know that one simple "Mama" would have sufficed. This explains the late night chatter I often hear coming from a bedroom where two young boys are supposed to be sleeping, and also explains the chatter we occasionally hear coming from the bathroom sink area where one little boy (very much alone) is having a conversation with the kid in the mirror.

Here is the kicker though: one day that blender gets turned off. A switch is flipped, or maybe a storm flips the breaker, and the hourglass in that boy's life is not being shaken anymore. It might still gently hum like your furnace in early spring, but it is no longer an incessant rattling from the old radiator. The sand in their hourglass begins to flow more slowly, the words are chosen more carefully, and inevitably those same boys now become *quieter*. From what I am told, that first slow down happens around age seven. I have read that they will become more introspective, more secretive, and have a greater tendency to hole up in their room with a good book or a box of Legos.

As our little boys become tweens, and then teens, when we really *need* them to start talking to us, they have just come to realize they had better start preservation mode. They have girls to woo, even job interviews to do and they really need to start being more selective about who and what their words are used on. This is subconscious and completely out of their control, of course. It also helps explain the cultural phenomenon of texting. It is word preservation at its finest. Fast forward twenty years and some of these young men will grow into adults labeled "men in their caves" by their wives, incapable of even the minimal amount of communication that the women in their lives hunger for. These poor guys have simply expended their lifetime allotment of words during early childhood. It's not their fault really, they simply talked, giggled and blabbered their way through most of their allotted words, right there with their mother standing by so many years ago.

But forgive me, I have strayed. Let's get back to naptime. Well, first let me admit that in addition to the reasons I previously stated about how much nicer it is for a baby to *complete* their nap, there is another reason why I so desire those boys of mine to be quiet while their sister is sleeping. (Warning!!! It is an entirely selfish reason.) When Brooklynn sleeps, the unadulterated fact is that I get to *sit down*. Or at least I plan to sit down. It does not always happen, but I like the option. Or maybe I have not showered in two days and a little clean up is in order. Again, I like to know that I have the option to perform the most basic of human hygiene. So when my boys decide to make use of their booming announcer's voices, my shower in all likelihood will be thwarted by a screaming baby girl.

We recently swapped this baby girl's crib out for a toddler bed, and although this is a grandly pivotal moment of babyhood colliding with childhood, it complicates the napping thing. Now, if she is woken up, she is literally *up*. Walking out her door, running down the halls, upset at the rude awakening and seeking solace in the arms of her mother. This of course is difficult to manage while said mother is buck-naked in the shower with a head full of conditioner. But let's be honest, even hygiene takes a backseat to my simple and pure desire to sit down when my baby is asleep. I want to sit and *do nothing*. I do not want to do email, I do not want to read a magazine, and I do not want to fold laundry. I just want to sit. My husband still cannot comprehend this phenomenon. In the off chance that I actually sit down in his presence, with the clear appearance of wanting to do nothing, he will still ask me, "What are you doing?" Please keep in mind that he says it in all innocence, he is not patronizing me. He just really wants to know. He simply cannot fathom sitting down for the sole purpose of sitting down. Bless his heart.

Having admitted my pure and simple desire to sit down and do nothing, I must say that it is not in my nature to do so. I have actually spent a good number of days in my lifetime being that ever busy, accomplished, if slightly procrastinating "Get-It-Done" type. Always working on at least two tasks, while planning the third, is how I am wired. Motherhood met me on my life's journey, however, highjacked my body, and ran me over one too many times. Since I have birthed and decided to keep my children, I have only had a few occasions to sit down. So I have come to value these occasions like a poor man values his last meal. Unfortunately, while in the throws of motherhood I have often overlooked these quiet and hidden opportunities to relax and I intend to start taking better inventory.

In order to actually find time to *just sit down* I have found that my gift of multi-tasking is priceless. I have the ability to talk on the phone while starting a load of laundry, feeding the dogs, filling out the homework reading log, taking out the garbage, all while drinking a cup of coffee and applying my lip gloss. Some people are blessed with this skill. Others are not. My husband is not. Brandon would never admit to not being capable of multitasking. He will just vehemently deny ever *wanting* to be able to do that kind of multitasking. Now, do not get me wrong. He is *always* busy, but always with *just one thing*. If he is seeding the lawn, he is not watching the children play in that very same lawn and most definitely did not see the dog tackle one of the children in the lawn. He might not even hear the child crying after the assault took place. Now I, on the other hand, can hear the dog approaching the child with a running, floppy, almost certainly dangerous glee while I am upstairs, in the house, on the phone. I call it "Mama Surveillance." I cannot explain it. I will not even attempt to explain the awesome importance of this inborn supervisory skill that I believe many mothers have and that somewhere in evolution was lost to the male species of our kind. But I still get pissed off when he cannot do it.

So if I get a chance to turn "Mama surveillance" down a notch, say, during Brooklynn's naptime, I am either twice as productive in my household responsibilities, or I am *sitting down*. Correction: Sitting down with that cup of coffee that I have warmed up for the twelfth time that day. I might even be holding a cookie. Or two. But that extra cookie is another chapter. Today, for quiet time, I have sent the boys upstairs to their room to play. They are far away from Brooklynn's room with the hope that if they do transmutate from best friends to worst enemies, Brooke may not have to hear it. Normally they are not allowed to be together for this very structured hour in our home, where books, puzzles (or if I am feeling exceedingly benevolent, the computer) will entertain them. Being together in their room was a special gift from their mother today, for good behavior earlier on. I started the practice of alone time when they were quite young and they could be placed on two blankets across the room from each other. Now they are in separate rooms normally, entertaining themselves without me and without each other. Bottom line, it is the time of day when I expect them to *just stop talking.*

Twin boys are inherently very good at entertaining themselves. Left to their own devices they can fill hours of playtime without a mothers input being needed at all. Many of my friends are quite jealous of this benefit of having twins. While they are consulting each other about yet another activity to engage their child in, I am watching my boys engaging in each other. I am told by other moms of multiples that this perk is truly only applicable to twin boys, and not other sets of twins. Girls tend to be more hypersensitive and therefore when a skirmish develops between two girl twins one of them will inevitably hold a grudge for the rest of the day over who got what doll, or which teacup goes with which saucer. Boys will be over it, literally, in seconds after the offending act took place. And of course, a boy and girl set of twins….well, most likely they are perfectly content not even knowing what the other twin is up to. Of course there are exceptions to these grossly simplistic descriptions, but I am still thankful that I have two babies who genuinely enjoy each other enough that they do not require my attendance in one hundred percent of their daily activities. Still, on most days quiet time is spent alone, without each other, and therefore can be actually quite calming.

So…here is my dream: The boys are on quiet time, Brooklynn is blissfully asleep, the dogs are resting wherever the beam of sunlight has moved to this time of day, and I am slowly lowering my backside onto the couch. Dream ends. The phone just rang. Forgive me, but I am one of those people who have been known to take advantage of my caller ID feature and elect to not take a call from time to time. (*Especially* if it is quiet time.) However, in order to utilize the caller ID, I still need to have the phone in my possession, so up with my bottom and into the kitchen I go. I chitchat for a few minutes with a friend, schedule a play date and bring the phone with me this time. I am actually sitting on the couch now. As I pause for a moment and hear nothing but the birds chirping outside, I joyfully reach for my coffee. Alas, the coffee is cold. Up with my bottom and into the kitchen I go. You can easily see how fast the precious quiet time can fly by.

Enter my dream sequence spliced with a hint of heaven: Ahhh….I now have a hot coffee cup in my hands, my backside is comfortable on the couch *and* I have a book in my hands. Now, you may think that the type of book is inconsequential. At least I get to read, right? Some of you may not even get that opportunity. But for me, the type of book is very significant. I am like my father and I have at least four books going at any given time. I might have a parenting book in my car, a political and/or professional read in the kitchen for over my breakfast, an inspirational book by my bed. For the all-valuable quiet time, I like to grab my "escape novel." In the past I have gravitated toward historical fiction. Romance and chivalry, set in Europe or somewhere else abroad that I have never traveled to are some of my favorites. No one told me you can actually learn history without memorizing dates, by the way. I discovered that on my own, thank you very much Mr. High School History Teacher. I find that historical fiction feeds the left half of my brain that wants to learn an interesting fact or truth that makes me wiser for having read it, while nourishing the right side of my brain that allows me to be distracted from my day-to-day responsibilities and dream up new possibilities and even improbabilities. More recently I have come to enjoy popular book club selections, bestsellers, and memoirs of women I can strongly relate to. Regardless of my current selection, reading my escape novels allows me a glimpse of something new and different without the drama of actually living it. It just does not get any better than that.

So there I am reading for the pure enjoyment of reading when all hell breaks loose. Quiet time isn't quiet anymore. Blake just realized that Tristan has a book that he wants and Tristan will not share it because he simply does not want to, which leads to Blake diverting his brother by suggesting a tryst into the bathroom where a "tea party" in the sink sounds like a good idea. (This is how quickly my boys can distract themselves.) Now, the only problem with this in all honesty is that the tea party will result in screams of delight and a flood out the door. The delight I deem as wonderful, even the flood I can work with as it can easily be remedied with a towel. It is really just the scream I have a problem with. And so I am jerked rudely back into reality where there is no circle of stones to transport me back to the eighteenth century where some Highlander is saving the day and there is defiantly no longer a secret spy mission in Sweden to keep up with.

Maybe tomorrow's quiet time will be quiet. But today I have to go liberate a little girl from her bedroom who just heard that there is a huge party going on in the bathroom, and she wants in on the fun.

chapter thirteen

when you give a kid a water hose...

Maybe you know the popular children's books written by Laura Numeroff that begin with something like, <u>If You Give a Cat a Cupcake</u>? The story goes that the cat will want sprinkles with that cupcake, which leads to sprinkles on the floor (of course), and then the sprinkles need to be cleaned up, and inevitably the child trying to meet the fantastical whims of her kitty is exhausted and asleep at the table. Children laugh when hearing these stories, thinking how crazy silly that kitty is. Their mothers want to cry, nodding like bobble head figurines, knowing all too well what it feels like try to please our little ones' often nonsensical impulses each day. You want to color with only pink markers tonight, sweetheart? Of course we can put away the others. You would like to eat dinner on the Nemo plate, and not that fully functional Winnie the Pooh plate I gave you? Oh, well, no harm in trading it out. You cannot find your shoes (because you did not put them into the shoe bucket when we came home)? Fine, flip-flops will be just fine since we need to be across town *TWO MINUTES AGO*. My poor mother-in-law could not figure out what Brooklynn was screaming about last summer when her breakfast was not quite right. Her brothers knew that she simply wanted a paper towel rather than a plate that morning. Simple, really.

Now some of you are shaking your heads thinking that my husband and I have *done it all wrong*. How can we allow our children to dictate such ridiculous specifics on the running of our household?! My answer is two-fold. First, I try to pick my battles. If my five-year-old is freaking out because I put spaghetti sauce on his noodles, and "You *know* I hate spaghetti sauce, Mom!" than I concede I made an error in my serving. A simple swap of plates will fix that misstep. A new dinner plate sans sauce is placed in front of him and dinner can resume. On the other hand, if that same five-year-old is freaking out because he does not want spaghetti for dinner and screeches that he wants a PB&J instead, he will get a look of stern correction and he will be asked if he would like to be dismissed from the dinner table. I will allow for distinct taste differences, I will not allow for rudeness.

Now, the second reason I tend to appease those oftentimes ridiculous requests that my children throw at me is because my father raised me while *listening to what I had to say.* My mother did not. She preferred it to be her way or the highway. Fast forward thirty years and I enjoy the company of my father more. In his own little way, he was showing me respect. He was recognizing that I had my own *agenda* you might call it. He was recognizing that there were things that I felt were important, maybe things I felt needed to be said or things I felt were important to do, and even things I felt were important to control. Earlier today when the children and I were all loaded into the car, pulling out of the driveway, Tristan exclaimed that he forgot his baby whale up in his room. At which point I calmly put the car into park, turned to him and reminded him that our newly created rule was that if you did not bring your toy into the car before your seatbelt was on, you were not allowed to bring it. Now this rule was created to prevent the very scenario that was occurring (the Oh, No! I Forgot to Grab My Toy panic that had been occurring much too frequently). He looked at me, his face distraught, recognizing that this new rule should probably apply to the situation at hand. But then his eyebrows briefly knotted together, his eyes got a spark of calculation in them, and he calmly stated, "Mom, my baby whale is *different* than a monster truck or a toy like Blakey brought. My baby whale is my *lovey*, and he would miss me today if I forgot him." Point taken. Leaving behind a lovey is for Tristan, akin to my leaving behind one of my children. "Now, quickly run upstairs and get your lovey so we can be on our way."

I recognize with 20/20 vision that I am making it more difficult on myself by allowing my children such freedoms as those written above. But I feel so strongly that I am encouraging independent thought, and in the case of my older boys, the skills of negotiation, that I will allow these liberties as much as I can. Quite frankly, Brooklynn especially, at two years old, is deserving of some control over her life. I mean if you think about how long she has been buckled, strapped and locked into one contraption or another it is eye opening. We bring them home from the hospital buckled into a three-point harness, at which point we lay them down in their cage - I mean crib. Then when they are a little older, they are strapped into the baby swing, baby bouncer, or baby snuggly until its mealtime and we lock them in their high chair. We may go for a walk but they are locked down into their stroller for that too. When tummy time and crawling get to be too much to monitor 24/7, we placed them in the other cage, otherwise known as a playpen. Come on folks, we can hardly fault them when they turn two years old and want to make a few decisions on their own. So they want to venture into otherwise unseen corners of the house, scale tall furniture with a single bound, and heaven forbid they want to chose their own breakfast bowl? A few allowances are really just the fair thing to do, don't you think?

You might call it "choosing your battles," I call it "endorsement." I endorse my children. I endorse their socially acceptable, politically correct qualities, *along with their peculiarities*. While writing this book I have found that my truest and most genuine desire for my family and for myself is to unconditionally love each other. You get what you give, and so I intend to dish it out to my fullest capacity and hope to receive it in return. That is not always the easiest thing to do, but it is my goal. By giving up the reins, I give up the notion of conformity. They do not need to be something they are not, or do something that defies their true nature. Nonconformity is a powerful lesson to teach your children. That they should not feel swayed to keep up with their peers and simply do what everyone else does will serve them well in the future. I want to teach them to be authentic to themselves and to love their uniqueness. I want to honor their dreams, their values and their goals. I want them to live deliberately (which is impossible for a child *not* to do, by the way) and enjoy the life journey they are on.

So let's get back to the moment that inspired this chapter, shall we? It is a typical Sunday afternoon, in springtime Georgia. The kids want to play, run, and spend much anticipated quality time with Daddy. Brandon happens to be washing his car on this beautiful day which just so happens to be one of Tristan and Blake's favorite household chores. To own their very own standard issue garden hose is probably on the top of their lifelong dreams list. Needless to say, these boys want in on the car washing. Daddy is busy finishing his own vehicle, cleaning the wheel hubs and such, and really does not want the hose run all over his car again, so he suggests that the kids wash Mommy's car instead. "That's a *GREAT* idea, Dad!" exclaims Tristan, and off he goes running with screams of delight. Five minutes go by, maybe ten. At some point Daddy decides it is too quiet over by Mama's car. Much to his dismay he finds his boys fitting the water hose up the tailpipe. Keeping his cool, he gently scolds them and explains that it is not appropriate or allowed to do such a thing. They listen to him immediately, pulling the hose away from the tailpipe, and Daddy goes back to his work.

A few hours later, the boys are all happily tucked into bed. Their skin is still cool to the touch, though dry, after hours of fun water sport in the driveway. My boys have been like little fish since the day they were born, always loving baths and any other form of water play, so this Sunday has met all of their greatest expectations for quality time with their Daddy. I sing them their songs, Skinna Ma Rink a Dinka Dink being the requested melody of the night. They listen contently, while I run my hand gently through their hair and down the sides of their faces. They yawn as the song closes, and they roll over on their sides pulling their blankies up tight under their chins. Tristan reaches up over the side of his bunk bed and gives me one of his big kisses and whispers that he loves me. Blake is already asleep. The adventure of the day is over and nighttime is calling and they are quite willing tonight for dreamtime to begin.

Twenty minutes later, I have gotten my things together for a rendezvous to a girlfriend's house. A new movie was just released onto DVD that I have been dying to see and she bought the movie. Though Sunday night is not my night of choice for a girls' night, I am not being fussy. I kiss my hubby goodnight, tell him it will be late when I get back and I head out the door. The first thing I notice is how clean my car looks. It is freshly washed, still wet in some places, and shinier than I have seen it in months. I look around and thankfully confirm that all of the windows were firmly shut while the hose was doing its thing. Good work, Daddy. I get in, and begin to readjust all of the buttons that my daughter has messed with while playing inside the car. Brooklynn is at this adorable age where she loves to sit in the driver seat and pretend she is taking her dolls for a trip. She buckles them into her car seat, crawls into the driver seat and begins the tedious task of moving mirrors, locking doors, adjusting the fan controls, turning the hazard light on and off, and even resetting the interior light intensity. (Please rest assured that all of this is done while the keys of the car are safely tucked away in the house.) It does mean, however, that after one of her joy rides I have some minor details to attend to, so I return the mirrors and controls back to their default positions, put the keys in the ignition and turn the key. The car does nothing. I try again, this time I get some sputtering, some gas gulping sounds and what sounds like gurgling from the back of the car. I give it another go, gun the accelerator and hear something that now sounds like a soda bottle tipped upside down emptying. With each *glug – glug* I get more nervous and realize I need to get my husband. With Brandon now in tow, I show him the unknown liquid dripping from the tailpipe and look at him completely perplexed. At which point, he hangs his head and says, "I thought I caught them *trying* to get the hose up there, not *finishing the job.*" Then he fills me in.

To remedy this new development, Brandon stands ten feet back from the muffler and I gun the accelerator again. The water shooting out of the tailpipe resembled turning on a fire hose. It took ten minutes and one trip around the neighborhood to empty the effects of two five-year-olds washing my car. I still made it to my girlfriend's house, and the kids were sat down the following day where it was reiterated that water hoses are not put up tailpipes. Looking into the future I feel certain that there will be many more scoldings for offenses that I cannot even dream of. Antics that only two boys, egging each other on, can concoct. My friend Laura has her own story written by *her* twin boys. It goes something like this: If you give a kid a nail clipper... he will clip his brother's eyelid off. Ouch. There was more blood associated with her adventure than with a water hose in a tailpipe. *I* avoided a visit to the ER. So it was a good day.

chapter fourteen

hey, do you want to warm me up?

It is a typical Sunday morning in our home and I am still lying in bed, having woken up relatively late. The alarm clock says it is eight o'clock, and I can hear the sounds of the kids' morning chatter with Daddy around the kitchen table. I could get up and join the festivities, but today I choose to keep my eyes closed and just listen to their banter. Most mornings at our home it is me in the thick of breakfast duty with three small children, buttering toast while checking for wet underwear while simultaneously trying to gulp down a coffee. I rarely have a chance to appreciate the morning discussions of a household dominated by humans that are four years and under, who are still wiping the sleep from their eyes. Usually it is me who greets them with hugs and kisses as they slowly crawl down the stairs, stuffed animals in hand. I am quite familiar with how it runs and what sort of things they expect from their morning. They want to play before they potty, they want to play before they dress and the only thing that can convince them otherwise is a promise of food. My husband, who leaves for work before the sun comes up during the work week is privy to this information however and is quite skilled on a Saturday or Sunday morning at convincing a Future Monster Truck Driver to stop and empty his bladder before it spills its contents out on its own. So today I choose to stay in my warm bed, with my covers pulled up to my ears, listening to the beautiful workings of the morning.

Brandon is one of those fathers that thoroughly enjoys these mornings with his kids, even if he gets flustered trying to appease every child's wish for this particular race car plate, or that particular dinosaur cup. There is no rush today to set out school uniforms or backpacks and there are no lunches to pack. The kids know that if Daddy is making breakfast they will get eggs, eggs and more eggs – a welcome treat from Mommy's cereal and milk. On occasion there is the loud exclamation, "No, Daddy. We wanted *sunshine* toast, not regular toast," but all in all Daddy hits the nail on the head and everyone's tummy is on its way to being pleasantly full. The conversation over the breakfast table inevitably turns to sports, as

Daddy usually has Sportscenter or ESPN on in the background. If there is a NASCAR race on later that day, I will overhear them discussing which car they want to win. Quite possibly there was a basketball game on the night before and Daddy is giving a thumbs-up or thumbs-down on the team's performance. The boys just eat this stuff up. So does his little girl.

If little Brooklynn, now two years old, so much as *sees* a basketball on TV or at a playground she will start jumping in her seat about "Da Da ball." You would think her father is an NBA star or basketball fanatic. He is neither. Brandon would never claim to love basketball more than say, football. In fact, there would be no competition between watching a Superbowl game or the NCAA tournament. He is a die-hard Green Bay Packer fan and would probably cut off his left arm to meet Brett Favre. The reason his little girl equates basketballs with her favorite person in the world is because of a church league he played in while she was only one year old. For three straight months she sat on the bleachers each Sunday with her brothers and I yelling, "Go Daddy!" She became more and more obsessed with basketballs as the weeks went by.

Anyone with a toddler knows how prevalent OCD is in these small children. Obsessive Compulsive Disorder seems to capture their little neurons one by one turning already self-absorbed munchkins into maniacal machines of greediness and adoration. Tristan and Blake at this age fell in love with trains. Brooklynn has gone head over heels for Ariel, pronounced "Oreo" in our home. She loves The Little Mermaid books, Ariel movies, dolls, paint sets, nightlights and jewelry. When we were at Panama City Beach on vacation, she requested we bury her in the sand and make *her* into a mermaid. She found a shell necklace at the local dollar store that looked just like the one Ariel wears and she wore it every day we were there. Walking down the aisle of our local bookstore, Target or even the grocery store, she will scream in delight if she sees Ariel on a package of panties, band-aids or even bath bubbles. Once we were ordering a muffin at the Atlanta Bread Co and she asked for an Ariel muffin. A fellow parent heard the request and laughed, as his daughter shared the same obsession. So this basketball obsession was nothing to be overly surprised about, but it sure did pull on Daddy's heartstrings. Brandon may not be a professional basketball player, but he was *Brooklynn's* basketball player. He bought her a little pink basketball, in appreciation for her unending love and support. From my hideout under the covers that Sunday, I could actually hear the smile on his face when she began her Daddy cheer during a basketball spot on ESPN.

When the eating had come to an end and I hear Daddy's sighs of disgust at the impending clean up necessary, I resolutely climb out of bed to join him. My hair is tousled and there are sleep lines still on my face. He has no idea I have spent the last twenty minutes just listening and appreciating my family. I welcomed the giggles, the bonding, the sweetness of time spent with a man that my children deserve to spend every waking moment with, but whom life's responsibilities steal from them five days out of the week. So on this precious Sunday morning, I start my day loving my children and adoring my husband even more than normal. Morning hugs from the kids and the questions of what I dreamed about the night before chase me around the kitchen while I fumble with my coffee cup and cereal bowl. I know that there is only a short period of time for this bliss of togetherness before the demands of the day set in. Showers, baths, church clothes and (God help me – literally this is a prayer to the Big Guy) shoes to put on, will soon encompass us while we prepare ourselves for the day. So I revel in this laxity of the moment and might even crawl onto my husband's lap for some quick morning chitchat. Ten minutes later however, the spell is broken, and time plays catch up. It is time to get down to business.

Having three small children to herd into church is no small feat. I know that other families appear to do it easily, though I suspect that in the confines of their home or minivan there were probably a few dramatic outcries or shouting matches. Every Sunday morning in our home, just after ten o'clock, the lazy morning fun is over and the pressure is on. Shoes, coats, one toy allowed for the ride, shoulder bag for books, a snack for the ride home, water bottles, and a coffee cup for Mama packed. Somewhere in the midst of this mayhem Daddy packs a wonderfully yummy and chocolaty protein bar for himself with every intention of eating it on the way there. Naturally, we are already out of the neighborhood when Brooklynn spots the gooey goodness and loudly announces that she too "wa a pobein ba!" Too late to turn back, too late to prevent the other two monsters in the back seat from hearing, and Daddy is short one delicious and nutritious mid-morning snack. The good news: we are actually on our way.

Pulling into the church parking lot, my parental expectations for the next ninety minutes begin to flow from my mouth like a gushing water tap. Admittedly loud and repetitive (and hugely overbearing in the opinion of my children), this last minute reminder of what kind of behavior we expect is absolutely necessary in order to create some semblance of order during our weekly Roman Catholic obligations. No, Blake you may *not* bring your monster truck in with you. No, Tristan you do *not* need to get a drink from the drinking fountain. No, Blake you may not dip your entire arm into the holy water font. No, Tristan you do not need to go the bathroom again. Wait…did you two go potty before we left the house? No??? Forgive me Father for I have sinned, we will be late *again*. And so at about 11:05am mass can begin because the Hellenbrand family has finally arrived:

The children are nestled all snug in their seats
With airplane books, Bibles and Brooklynn's dolly at her feet.

For thirty whole minutes Mommy and Daddy are shocked,
The kids are so sweet and their mouths have been locked.

They're sharing their books, they are standing and kneeling
And all around us the people are happy and cheering.

When what to our wandering eyes should appear
But one quick little scratch on one cute little ear.

Brooklynn's nails have done damage, Tristan's fast to react
Her doll gets a kick and the doll takes a smack

And so in one moment, the sweetness is gone.
And Brooke is hauled out of the church during a song.

We'll survive it, we know it, (we usually do.)
The boys have been good though- success out of the blue!

So we head out the door, just right after mass,
The reward for two four-year-olds having some class?
Happy Sunday to all, Dunkin Donuts at last.

Driving home with sticky fingers and remnants of pink sprinkles on my children's faces, the feeling of success and relaxation slowly seeps into my blood stream. Even the children are showing signs of a quiet satisfaction. Blake's head is resting contentedly on his car seat and Tristan is asking if it is quiet time when we get home. Even little Brooklynn agrees that naptime sounds like a fine idea. The pace of life on a Sunday *should* be slow and deliberate, I think. It is a Day of Rest. Thinking back to my earlier driving days I remember complaining about all of those "Sunday drivers" who were slowing me down. Now at the ripe old age of thirty-two, however, I get it. We file into the house one by one, zombie-like. The boys head straight for their cars or whales, to play quietly upstairs in their room. Brooklynn goes to her room to look for her favorite pink shorts that are her mandatory napping attire. Daddy heads for the kitchen to find protein to supplement his missed snack. And Mommy? I may or may not find myself making lunch. Today we ate enough donuts to fill us up for a while and lunch can wait. My to-do list can wait, it will be here tomorrow. So without any guilt at all, I grab my book and sit down in the sun to read.

Something about a sunny spot *indoors* feels so coveted and special. Dogs crave them and lounge there for hours if left to their own devices. I am not sure if it is the vitamin D penetrating into my skin that makes me feel so happy and content, or if it is because at this hour of the day I am allowed to assume the much needed *siesta* position that those folks south of us recognize as necessary for survival. Inevitably one of the boys will crawl into my lap or lie on the couch and crash into dreamland. It is all so hypnotic and lovely and good. Only eight *short* minutes later however, Tristan discovers his brother blissfully asleep on the couch, at which point he decides to steam roll over him, giggling madly. At about that same time Daddy decides it is time for some NFL Football highlights and I realize that it is in my best interest to have a hit of caffeine in order to keep up with it all.

Coffee, oh sweet coffee. It keeps me awake when I am sleepy and keeps me grounded when I am cranky. It keeps me warm when I am cold and it keeps me company when I am lonely. In short, a coffee cup in my hand is like a cig for a smoker. Consuming it is oftentimes optional, I can nurse one cup of coffee for hours. I enjoy the feel of the warm cup in my hands on a cold day, or even a mildly warm one. All year long it is a companion to my morning magazine or evening novel. My favorite flavor is vanilla nut, but any variety will do. I will drink it watered down (as in my college days) or as thick as motor oil at my brother-in-laws. I drink it in the morning and I drink it in the afternoon. I can drink it right before bed and still sleep like a log. The only time I have not consumed coffee was when I was trying to get pregnant, was pregnant, or was nursing. When I gave it up, I swear I had withdrawal headaches for at least a week. It is ironic really, because I consider myself a pretty healthy person. I carefully watch what my children eat, *obsessively* some would say. I made all their baby food from scratch with only the best organic fruits and vegetables. They were given bottles of water to drink rather than milk or juice and I still puree spinach or raspberries into their brownies. I buy all natural peanut butter, refuse to drink soda or anything with aspartame or Splenda in it and pride myself in the healthy snacks I send with them to school. I try to shop in the outer aisles of the grocery store and buy limited quantities of processed foods. My children do not know what Lucky Charms or Fruity Pebbles are (and seem just as excited about Blueberry Clusters in their cereal bowl). When we visit Papa Roger in Montana, the very idea that it is okay to eat Cocoa Krispies for breakfast (and that there are *toys!* in the boxes) is enough excitement to carry them for days. Through the years as our kids have gotten older, we have gotten more lax on some of the particulars. We *do* eat ice cream, we just buy Breyer's All Natural. (I feel comfort knowing that there is actually cream in our ice cream.) There are other allowances we have made, and food items we are adamantly against. If the maple syrup does not come from a tree, we are not buying it. Few know the ingredient list on an Aunt Jemima bottle, I suggest reading it. My sister-in-law, Heather had a household rule allowing each child one sweet per day. We have adopted that rule here and there. Syrup counts by the way.

I concede that my addiction to coffee does not seem to meld with my philosophy on living a healthy life. It is in direct conflict with what I believe and what I know is best for me. I am a hypocrite at their worst because every time I see someone at the checkout counter at the grocery store with Pop-Tarts, Popsicles, and Capri-Sun on the conveyer belt, I admit that I cringe. In my own shopping cart, however, two bags of coffee, sometimes artificially flavored, sit for purchase. I would like to apologize for being *that* person. Enjoy your Pop-Tarts, because I will enjoy my Starbucks.

So this Sunday afternoon, sitting in my sunny chair next to the window, I am holding my coffee and completely engrossed in a good book. My little Brooklynn is now sleeping in her pink little bed in her pink little room wearing her pink little shorts, to the sounds of lullabies piping through her radio. Tristan and Blake, both awake now, are up in their bedroom pounding on Hungry Hungry Hippos as loud as they can. Brandon is watching his sports update while catching up on Quick Books and our budget. It is a beautiful, sunny, lazy Sunday. As it should be.

Ten minutes go by, twenty, thirty. My coffee is now cold since I am so wrapped up in my book. Brandon stands up to go get something from the kitchen and I innocently say to my husband, "Hey Hon, would you warm me up?" He grins. Big. Ear to ear. God help me, he does not see the coffee cup. Does not even register that I am handing him something that needs to be heated. His brain just knows that his ears heard something *very* interesting. More interesting than ESPN. And at least for the briefest of seconds, he thinks I have just thrown out a pick-up line for a quickie. I honestly cannot help but chuckle as he remembers that "warm me up," is coffee lingo for "throw it in the microwave, please." He laughs too, but I know that for the rest of this wonderful Sunday afternoon he will be suffering from a disappointment that only a man can know on such an otherwise perfect Sunday.

A perfect day. Not because the children did not squabble with each other. They have. Not because meal preparation was handled by Daddy and Dunkin Donuts, though it was. Perfect, because we are together. Perfect, because we have no responsibilities other than those to each other. The best part is that there are still *hours* left to this day, and each delicious hour has a lot of potential. Maybe we will carve pumpkins or go for a neighborhood stroll. A family game of Candy Land, a hot supper in our tummies and the kids will be put to bed early, as on every Sunday. I am thirty-two years old and I readily admit that I am now the Sunday driver, the Sunday cooker (donuts for lunch!), the Sunday housewife (the chores can wait!) and the Sunday Mom (sure, we can play another game of checkers!). Quite possibly I will end this day as the Sunday Good Wife and ask my spouse for a little warm up, literally this time.

chapter fifteen

hide-and-seek on a forty-foot sloop

This past summer I acquired a nickname that I am not entirely proud of. Though "beach whore" immediately brings to mind smutty inferences that in my case are *without a doubt false* (get your head out of the gutter), when loosely applied to the frivolous acceptance of many-a-invitation to various beach houses owned by persons other than myself, I suppose it applies. One of my dearest friends Laura and her husband Brad bestowed this nickname on me while we were all seated on their family's Orange Beach pier, sipping Whisky Willy's margaritas, watching a gorgeous Gulf shore sunset.

Beginning around April this year, when the sun still sat quite low in the sky and when the wonderful possibilities of summer had yet to show their little buds, we had already begun our monthly treks to the beach. My husband and I, with kids in tow, took the family to the North Carolina Outer Banks area, having been invited there by one of Brandon's sisters. A five-bedroom house a stone's throw from the Atlantic Ocean complete with two decks, a surplus of sand toys for the kiddies, and several Parties in a Bucket for us parents, promised a fun weekend for all. It did not disappoint. We had a beautiful vacation spent in the sand and on the water and although we were blessed with perfect weather for various beach activities such as romantic walks on the beach, lazy baking in the sun, and quiet nights falling asleep listening to the waves, none of these things actually came to fruition.

With seven children between our two families (half of them being five years old and under), the little people actually outnumbered the big people and therefore the big people spent most of their days *head counting*. Seven heads still running on the sand? Check. Seven heads still above water in the waves? Check. Seven heads at the dinner table? Check. Still, any parent knows that as soon as the children outnumber the adults there is bound to be trouble, and that expectation *did* come to realization. With six kids piled into one small bathtub, four kids buried in the sand with sand buckets over their heads, and two toddlers who seemed drawn to the tide with the lunar pull, it was a vacation that was part beach fun and mostly hard work. If at any time we felt the incurable itch to kick our feet up and read a novel, my nephew Caden would very quietly open up the refrigerator and empty out its contents, adults be damned. We celebrated each day that we all survived by eating entire packages of Oreo cookies and putting the kids to bed at 6:30pm. (Well, *my* kids were tucked in anyway.) At the conclusion of the long weekend, we assessed our surprise vacation and decided definitively that we had had a wonderful time, and all for the small price of *nothing.* Zero dollars. Roxanne would not allow us to contribute to the beach house. We may as well have been hobos up from Georgia to crash their vacation. They were overly generous and we felt blessed to have joined them.

Shortly after that first trip to the beach we began our regular excursions to Orange Beach, Alabama with Laura and Brad. Laura comes from a very large family in Alabama and her parents helped the family purchase a large home on one of their beautiful bays, with the understanding that the lower level of the beach house must always be open for family to come and enjoy the bay waters, sailing, and original artwork on display. Laura's sister Teresa and her husband Willy have taken up permanent residence there and are the hosts for all Furman family holidays. Whiskey Willy is first an alcohol extraordinaire, having his own brand of margaritas, bloody Mary's and other concoctions I highly suggest you try. Second, he is a yard art/wall art Picasso, having adorned his home and yard with a multitude of artistic pieces that make his abode feel like a tiki hut right out of Key West. Lastly, the man is a terrific host. He and Teresa, along with their two boys have opened their home to us now three times and almost always bring food and drink downstairs to share with whoever is invading their home *this* particular weekend. There are a couple different sail boats docked outback, a fishing boat, a little catamaran for joyriding, along with beautiful views of "Pirate Island" – an uninhabited stretch of land across the bay that we have named for our boys to enjoy testosterone-filled adventures. Have I mentioned that these wonderful friends of ours have twin boys the same age as our twin boys? Mark and Adam are full of life and laughter and a fair share of testosterone. Other than being very, very loud, they are some of the sweetest little boys I have ever meet. I have watched our two boys with their two boys marching into church together with long lopey gaits, arms swinging, carting a various collection of stuffed animals to include a trout fish, a baby brontosaurus, a bat and a hammerhead shark. I could not help but think of the movie Stand By Me when those boys were marching down the railroad track to the tune of

"Have Gun Will Travel." It is quintessential boyhood in the making right there. Not only do Laura and Brad have a set of twins whose preferences and behavior often mirror my own boys', but they also have a little girl named Maggie who is only a year younger than my little Brooklynn. The two girls can play for hours with little princess toys or even fishing poles, and for the most part they get along splendidly. Little Maggie, being only two years old will eventually exhaust herself and regress to pulling Brooke's hair or throwing the toys across the room, but thankfully each month that passes by there is less and less of this drama. Brooklynn has endless patience so it all works out.

So far this summer we have had a tremendous time on our trips to Orange Beach. We frequent the Gulf shoreline, playing "Goggle Monster" where one lucky daddy is designated the monster and the kids all try to climb on top of him and sink him. This singular activity can fill a good forty minutes of our trip to the beach, after which the designated daddy generally collapses on the sand, a five-star workout accomplished. The girls bury their legs in the sand and call themselves mermaids, and once again the mommies are in charge of head counting and photographing these playful, fun moments. On several occasions we have been lucky enough to go out on a sailboat for trips to Pirate Island or simply to dolphin watch. Herb, Laura's father has his own sailboat docked at Willy's and he has been so generous as to take us out for a peaceful sail around the bay. Brooklynn saw her first dolphin, swimming only eight feet off the starboard, and Brandon got the first itch to learn more about the sport of sailing while enjoying the calm, cool breezes off the water. The last vacation we took down there we actually spent the night on Brad's sailboat, named "Twinscape." The name of his boat is sort of a sticking point for Laura and Brad, as you might imagine, but it is a beautiful forty-foot long sloop, with a nice size cabin that the five of us could comfortably sleep in. Of course, what Blake and Tristan found most appealing about the entire experience had little to do with the sleeping arrangements, onboard air conditioning, or gentle sway of the boat. "We can go potty on this thing too, Mom!" It turns out that the ability to urinate on a boat is actually the requirement for boat "coolness" in the mind of newly six-year-old young men.

I cannot stress enough how much we appreciate our extended Orange Beach family. The first time we went down Laura felt she needed to prep me for the humble establishment which is their second home each summer. Willy and Teresa's home looks like many of the homes down there, towering three stories tall with porches on each level. Every level of their home is very unique, architecturally speaking, with a professional grade kitchen (to aid in Whisky Willy's newly dreamed concoctions I suppose), huge open rooms, connected by an almost maze of hallways and small utility rooms. Most of the features that stand out in their home were hand built, lovingly painted or sanded by Willy himself. The beach access level, the lowest level, is where we hang our hats and spend our time when we visit. It is decorated a-la-Willy style. As I mentioned, he is a creative sort who likes to put his personal touches throughout the space and I suspect that Teresa gives him his most creative freedom on the lower level. Lime green walls, various liquor paraphernalia, boatyard art, fish mirrors, and a very bare bones kitchen with a stove that actually threatens to take our lives each visit with its electrical short on three of the four burners. The bottom cabinets are made from cinder blocks and I was told that this is because they had water damage following one of the recent hurricanes that came through the area and nothing can damage cinder blocks, right? I think it is clever. The mattresses probably date back to the eighteen hundreds and there is only one window-installed air conditioner on the entire floor (which still manages to freeze me out of the house each visit since the men set it to the frigid setting). I laugh when Laura still feels the need to point out each cosmetic pimple in the place because it is a *beach house.* It is more beach house than I currently own and more than I will probably *ever* own. So I am extremely grateful to these friends who share their good fortune and good family with us.

Having said that, I must share my very real concern that Laura and Brad feel "cheated on," earning me the nickname. Earlier this summer another friend of mine by the name of Laura (yes confusing, we will call her Laura B) invited my kids and me down to Destin, Florida for a couple days. She and her husband purchased a beach house late last year and she was spending most of the summer down there with her kids, leaving her husband to his oncology work in Georgia. This is a newly discovered benefit to living in Georgia, as my Wisconsin friends and family will never experience the bliss of traveling only five hours by car to spend a few days on the ocean. So the offer seemed too good to pass up. We had a fabulous time in Destin. Her home is also three stories, five bedrooms and right next to the beach. The difference is that her home is a decorator's dream. It looks like it is straight out of an Ethan Allen catalog, and clean enough that I would literally feel comfortable licking my dinner off of her floor. In contrast, the Orange Beach place most definitely requires dinnerware, copious amounts of hand sanitizer and that is only if the stove has not killed you by day two. Oh, and might I mention that Laura B.'s Destin place overlooked what was rumored to be Faith Hill's new beach house? A different class of beachfront living, I suppose. In reality both of my "Laura friends" are wonderful women that are more alike than they are different. Both women are raising kids that enjoy running, screaming, and generally *being* kids. Both women provide a relaxing, drink-in-hand ambiance at the end of the day when the kids are finally in bed, and most importantly both of these women can be counted on for some first-rate girl talk. Even so, my Orange Beach Laura felt a little insecure after hearing about my new beach accommodations in Destin. Bless her heart.

This summer is very quickly ending and it has brought me to my knees at times, in reflection of what wonderful friends and family we have in our lives. The experiences that we are having this year are new for my children but also new for Brandon and I. Never did we imagine ten years ago that we would get to spend vacations with family on the beach every summer. Thanks to Brandon's workplace condominium in Panama City Beach, we have spent the past decade meeting various family members for weeklong escapes to the beach. And even this year, when the condo was no longer a luxury that Brandon's employer could afford, we were instead invited to North Carolina, Orange Beach, and Destin.

I sat on the Orange Beach pier this past Sunday morning holding a cup of coffee, enjoying the cool breeze off the bay, watching the four boys play on Brad's sailboat. They were playing hide-and-seek. Two boys were counting while climbing around on the deck of the boat, while two boys hid somewhere deep in the bowels. All of them traversed the terrain of the boat as if they were naturals, born on the water. I think that at this age they do not (and most likely, *cannot)* appreciate that most young men do not get to play hide-and-seek on a forty-foot sailboat on Gulf waters. The only thing they know is that they are with their best friends playing an old favorite game, and that they feel tremendously happy. Call me a beach whore if you want, but I am the most grateful, appreciative one you will ever find. I hope that my thankfulness rubs off on our kids. I hope that one day they will know how lucky they are to have had these experiences, these friends and these sunny days together.

chapter sixteen

pilot lessons & a brain aneurysm

So I am on Facebook now. My husband finds this hilarious and
wants to know how many *friends* I have. The truth is I have too
many. So many that I find it difficult to keep up with the ones I really
want to stay in touch with. Only a few years ago I relied on phone calls
to keep in touch with people, if you can still imagine that. I am not a
phone talker, however and Facebook has allowed me to come to peace
with that. I do not have the time or stamina to spend an hour on the
phone with someone. Between old Wisconsin friends, new Georgia
friends and the mandatory family members, I was failing miserably at
the art of staying in touch. Weeks would go by, then months, and
eventually I became the person who nobody heard from. Ever. So
began the period of my life when I was probably on everyone's shit
list. For about five years I can honestly say that I was off radar
entirely. You could not find me if you tried. I was running my
chiropractic office, out marketing my office, out marketing someone
else's office, dragging my munchkins around town in a mad desire to
spend quality time with them, cleaning, cooking and trying to squeeze
in some exercise on the side. So ultimately, to the rest of the world, it
appeared that I was gone.

Fast forward to today and my boys are almost five years old now,
Brooke is out of diapers, and I have officially parked my stealth plane
and can be located on the world map again. My office is sold and the
kids are old enough and disciplined enough to recognize nap time or
quiet time in our home. This all elusive hour, otherwise known as
"Mommy Hour," commonly finds me either comatose on the couch
dreaming up an IV unit to get caffeine into my system faster, sitting in
my favorite chair cozying up with my favorite book, or on my laptop
being social. I love Facebook because I can ignore it for weeks and
still catch up on one rainy afternoon with everyone that I truly want to
catch up with. I can see pictures of my girlfriend doing the "polar
plunge" that crazy Wisconsin people are so famous for. I can locate an
old friend from college that I have not seen in twelve years and read
about her travels around the world. I can see that another old friend of

mine is cleaning up puke yet again today, as her third child has just come down with the flu. I can chat with a local friend and plan a coffee date with her later in the week and laugh hysterically at my sixth grade class photo from twenty years ago that a high school acquaintance posted for all to enjoy. I can post embarrassing photos of my sister-in-law at our most recent New Years Eve celebration, knowing full well there will be hell to pay for it. (Nine hundred miles between us, be damned.) I can network with colleagues and schedule marketing engagements with another chiropractor in town. I can join online groups that I care about, like "No to Mandatory Vaccinations" while simultaneously spreading what I feel to be an important message to my friends. It is wonderful and at the end of it I feel so productive and caught up.

My lovely husband thinks this is all silly and refuses to have a Facebook account, of course. Quite frankly we share so many friends that I can just cut and paste what he would like to hear over dinner together, and leave out the rest. Recently however, something funny happened. A silly Facebook tag brought us closer to each other. It started with my receiving a post from my girlfriend Jackie that was titled, "25 random things about me." We have all gotten emails like this and nine times out of ten I skip them for later, skim them, or (apologetically, mind you) delete them. But Jackie is my girl. She is hilarious and painfully honest at times and I was curious what random things she would choose to share with twenty-five Facebook friends. So I read it. Three times. I laughed at a couple entries, my jaw dropped for others. I can honestly say that five of her twenty-five things were complete news to me, and this is a friend that I have known for fifteen years or more. It was great fun and I felt like a better friend to her for having read it. This person, who had seemed so transparent to me, is clearly more complex and mysterious than I gave her credit for. It was wonderful. So then I started writing my own 25 random things.

While I was creating my list I realized how much more difficult it was than I thought it would be. I wanted to share something of myself that I knew I did not share very often. And when I was finished, I felt protective of it. I was not sure I should share it. Certainly, I was unsure of who should read it. One person however, whom I felt should definitely know what I had written was Brandon. When we were finally sitting down together and he read it, there were things on it that charmed him and others that perplexed him. It was nothing new to hear about my desire to horseback ride in Ireland, but zip lining through a jungle was something he would not have pegged me for. He, of course, recognizes how much I love my children, but had no idea that on most days I consider the three of them my best friends. Owning a mini-van was never at the top of my to-do list but he had no idea that I am counting the days until I can have a cool car again. A red one. Mind you, these are not life altering discoveries though a few things on my list revealed more of my heart than I commonly like to. One of the more difficult things to put down was just how much I want to like my mom. I have an obligation to love her of course, but I just wish I could like her more. Poignantly put, Brandon said. So in the end, I asked Brandon to write *his* 25 random things. Though I suspect he was intrigued by the idea, he was uncomfortable with it. In fact, it took him a full week to put the list together and in the end he presented me with a list of 33 things. (He got carried away apparently and just could not contain or prioritize the last eight, so he left them all there.) During our Valentine's Day dinner date he presented me with the list.

You have to keep in mind that Brandon is a pretty elusive guy, in my opinion. He claims to be simple (actually stating as much as his #16 entry), as most men do, but that is only because *he* knows what is running through that head of his. The rest of us are quite puzzled, his wife in particular. So this was a big deal. I was finally getting inside his head without having to *drag* the information out piece by piece. Here it was, in a non-threatening, non-argumentative manner, laid out in black and white on the table. In English, no less, so miscommunication was impossible. I was free to discuss and clear up any questions I had right then and there. Wow, I am still amazed sitting here now, weeks later.

So what did he share with me? These were random things remember. Yet many of them were insightful and inspiring. Things that as his wife, I should know. Like how much he enjoys the beach, feeling the sand between his toes, and the ability music has to pull him out of a downward spiral on a bad day. Or how much he enjoys hearing his boys laugh, giggle and run around, exhibiting so much life and energy. Some were things I felt ashamed for not knowing (*he wants pilot lessons?!?!)* while others revealed hurts and sadness that had never been outwardly expressed until now. For example, his disappointment and sadness when his father chose to no longer be a Brett Favre fan. Bonding with his dad over one of his childhood heroes was something Brandon would sorely miss. On a lighter note, with his sense of humor shining bright, he addressed this "list nonsense" quite eloquently listing his #1: "Can you sell a wife on craigslist?" His #2 read: "If so, I would buy her back in a second."

These exercises in opening up to each other seem few and far between sometimes. Oh, we will talk about the kids, household responsibilities, and even work sometimes. However, if we stray too far into territory that has not been broached in awhile or God forbid, we disagree on the topic we are speaking of, Brandon has a habit of checking out. His eyes glass over, he starts looking for the kids so he can perform some dire parental responsibility that we must be overlooking and he exits the room. Last week we were talking about what it will be like when our boys are teenagers. Our nieces and nephews are fast approaching those exciting and yet terrifying years and I was speculating whether or not our boys would be expected to have jobs. My husband however, sensing a possible disagreement on the horizon, envisioning the responsibilities of football practice or other extra-curriculars possibly prohibiting a job, decides it is safer to *not go there*. Given that our boys are currently four years old, I find it ridiculous that we cannot both be assumed to have the rightness of mind to postpone an all out fistfight over the topic, but regardless the conversation was over. I felt so incredibly alone while I sat at the table post "almost conversation." I calculated the approximate number of hours that Brandon and I had spoken that day, revised it to *minutes* and realized that even though it was a Saturday and he had been home with us all day, our actual minutes of what I would consider adult conversation, tallied up to less than ten. In contrast, Tristan and I had logged in a good sixty minutes of quality "Mama I *love* this date" conversation. See, four-year-olds can talk your head off, and two-year-olds can babble your head off. Just rarely about politics, recent events, or dreams for the future. My children's only dream is that I will call them back to the table for a surprise ice-cream sandwich.

So I have decided that I want more of this closeness, this sharing of ideas, of dreams between the two of us. I want to know what moves him, what pisses him off, what keeps him getting up each morning. This past Christmas we were faced with one of our best friends, *thirty-two years old* almost dying of a brain aneurysm. There was no warning, no injury, and no predisposition to such a thing. It just happened. He has a young wife and two young children and he almost died. Just. Like. That. Just like that we can lose the ability to share this stuff with the people we love. And just like that I scheduled a trip to the British Virgin Islands for some beach, some boat, some sand, some music, for no better reason than to celebrate our tenth wedding anniversary.

Quality time is hard to find when you are parenting. Juggling it with your own need for personal time is even harder. In the midst of wanting to raise our children the best we can, we oftentimes forget to nurture what started it all. No one can deny that we change as the years go by. The qualities and interests that initially brought Brandon and I together may not be what keeps us together. A hefty dose of acceptance of this fact, along with hearty attempts to find new and unique ways to connect are the only way you can come out of parenting with your marriage still intact. Pilot lessons, huh? Go for it.

chapter seventeen

you can ask Ed

When I stop to reminisce about how this family of mine got started it is hard to believe that it has been almost sixteen years that my husband and I have been together. That is remarkable given that we are only thirty-two years old. Had I known at the young age of seventeen that the fate of my life rested on one prom date decision, I would have chickened out, of course. But life has a funny way of sneaking up on us, with surprises around every bend. My current residence, almost nine hundred miles from any living relative still comes as a shock to me from time to time. Certainly my twins were a surprise, and baby number three as well. There are small things too, that give me pause from time to time. This former pre-med student now waives vaccinations, and foregoes well-baby visits for my kids. With a doctorate in my back pocket, I find myself taking care of my children and my home rather than patients at an office. I am writing a book, for goodness sakes. That will forever be a surprise to me. My husband, who was told by his high school career counselor to go to a tech school rather than a four-year college, in the past twelve years has worked his way up from being an entry level engineer to managing the entire department of mechanical engineers at his corporation. He is able to be the sole financial supporter of his family and I believe he takes a lot of pride in that. Rightfully so, since it was implied to him by a guidance counselor that it would probably not go that way. The reality of course is that every couple on this planet has been surprised and has felt in awe of what has come their way. We each have a "story of us." This chapter reveals how fate, hard work and trust in something bigger and better brought about some of the best moments of our lives together. We could not have dreamed this big, hoped for so much, let alone had the foresight to make it all happen in such a beautiful way. I want to share with you how it all began.

I was seventeen years old when Brandon and I went on our first date. We were both juniors at a high school in a small town in Wisconsin. Our Junior Prom was fast approaching and my longtime girlfriend Sarah and I were discussing whom we wanted to go with to the dance. We were not members of the popular crowd, neither were we athletic stars or full-blown band geeks. Looking back I would categorize us in the Foolishly Naïve and Most-of-the-Time Nice group. We decided quite early not to wait around for an invitation to the dance. We decided to do the asking. The two guys we had our sights on were still available, happened to be best friends, and therefore a double date would in all likelihood be welcomed. Enter Brandon and Ed. Trying to decide who would ask who was one of those careful dances between friends that can either create a chasm of hurt feelings or a bridge of loyalty. When Sarah admitted that she did in fact have a preference, I let her choose first. She chose Ed.

There are a few things that I remember about that night as if it were yesterday. I remember thinking that Brandon had a huge and very loud family. Brandon has five siblings and he is one of the younger ones. His parents had just built a new house - literally- the walls were unfinished drywall with creative ramblings written all over them. There were measurements for future build-ins, ideas for paint or wallpaper designs, even funny messages his sister Tiffany had not realized would be on display for every guest that entered their home. The rooms were filled with very modest furniture, some so faded they looked to have lived on a porch in their previous life. Those pieces however, sat next to very beautiful antique furniture clearly passed down for generations and in impeccable shape. What I remember most about that first time I met his family however, is the look on his father's face when we were introduced. He shook my hand, looked me up and down and gave me a wide Irish smile.

I wore a beautiful hand sewn blue velvet dress. It was a gift from a woman who had become quite dear to me in those difficult teenage years and I felt like a movie star when I wore it. Brandon also looked the part, as dapper as could be in a tuxedo with a matching blue cummerbund that made his blue eyes sparkle. With his wide shoulders and combed hair, he looked quite striking. I caught his father looking at him as if he had never seen his son before that day.

A few exhilarating hours later, after many photographs and an Italian dinner with eight of our closest friends, my most vivid memory of the entire evening was dancing with Brandon. *Closely.* Not because I was particularly taken with this guy yet, although he had proven to be a great choice as prom dates go. No, we were dancing so close because he had decided *he was taken with me*. Being wrapped in his arms, swaying back and forth to one of Journey's greatest hits, I remember being thankful for being female, as we can be much more discreet about our feelings than the typical male teenager's anatomy allows for. If I danced with my girlfriends that night or giggled and gossiped, I can honestly say I have little recollection of it. This seems strange to me now, that the girls that shaped my entire high school experience up to that point were just backdrops in my memory of the evening. The last thing that really stands out in my mind is falling asleep on the floor at a friend's house afterwards. Yes, the guys were there. This was not, however, a hot and heavy *un*supervised post-prom party. Remember, I was one of the nice, naïve girls. No, we were at a completely supervised post-prom event, watching a movie while my girlfriend's parents discreetly made sure we were all behaving ourselves. I fell asleep on the living room floor next to Brandon, and when I woke the next morning my head was resting comfortably on his arm. His very numb arm, he admitted later. *Years later.* It turns out that his arm had been killing him all night long while supporting the weight of my head and that by morning he had what felt like phantom pains from a limb long since dead. But that sweet guy did not want to wake me up so he suffered through the night selflessly. If I had known that then, I would have known he was keeper.

Brandon was a football player, but not as rough around the edges as some of them. He was a jock, but with a sweet, quiet side. He was simple, wearing Waunakee Warrior football t-shirts and Levis jeans to school. A head full of hair, with cowlicks directing the show, he was quiet around my friends and family, but came out of his shell when surrounded by his own friends. Conversation between the two of us came easy. At the end of a school day I would curl up in my bed with the phone under my head talking to him until one or both of us fell asleep. And because I knew I would see him the next day at school, I could not wait for morning to come.

In short, I fell hard. So hard that my girlfriends thought I was crazy and so hard that this "good girl" realized it was hard to always be good. Looking back on those years, I do not regret any decisions I made. Yes, we were young. I was seventeen when I lost my virginity to my husband. My friends swore up and down that between the fact that my parents were divorced and that I was having sex with my boyfriend, I was certain to become a statistic as a pregnant teenager who was ruining her future. One friend felt so strongly about it that we stopped speaking later that year and have yet to speak a word to each other since. My other two closest friends simply drifted away in their life's direction while I did the same. Yet through all of that, Brandon was a constant.

We had seven years of ups and downs in our dating relationship. The early love characterized by infatuation and lust was followed by the more tumultuous time of living two hours apart for four years of undergraduate school. Though we occasionally were distracted by the waves, Brandon and I tumbled together like shells on a beach, enjoying the same stretch of sand over and over again. I declared myself pre-med at the University of Wisconsin-Madison while he was two hours away seeking an engineering degree. He came home every weekend to see me for *four years*. He told his friends that there was no better place to be on a weekend than at the University of Madison and its "party school" atmosphere. But in truth, he came up every weekend because I was there waiting for him. Two nights each week I got him back in my life, only to say goodbye again each Sunday. Early on in our college days we would spend those two nights partying into the wee hours of the night at some frat party or house party, waking up hung over and pitiful the next morning, reeking of stale beer and spilled wop (or jungle juice as they call it in the south). Later in our college career I asked if we could spend some "quality time" together one night each weekend and party on the other night. He agreed, if grudgingly. I believe that his consent was another pivotal point in our relationship where our love grew into a new, more mature one. Did we really *love* each other then? Yes, undeniably. Is it the same kind of love that we have now? No, of course it is not. It is however the same kind of love that anyone reading this recalls about their first love. It was beautiful and innocent and completely all encompassing. We were fearless and reckless and having the time of our lives.

Fast-forward seven years and in 1999, we tied the knot. I know, I know...how many girls do you know that wait around for seven years for a commitment? Well, I was young and more patient apparently than I am now. And he showed his commitment to me in visiting every weekend and spending summers at my apartment with me. God bless my roommates for silently agreeing to allow a fourth person to cohabitate with us for three months of the year. God bless Brandon's parents for making sure he had a car to make the trip up each weekend and for not asking too many questions about where he stayed. And God bless my father who recognized a reasonably mature adult in that young, crazy daughter of his.

Now, please do not assume that Brandon and I have had one of those soul-mate relationships that seem to navigate the sea of love with no rough waves in sight. In fact, there were tsunami-like waves that ripped us apart and tossed us back on shore gasping for air. My college roommates, many of whom are still some of my best friends to this day can attest to a few wild and senseless brawls between the two of us. Some of them were meaningless and long ago forgotten. Others were quite hurtful and have been forgiven, if not forgotten. I believe that to this day both Brandon and I wish we could just make the memories of those missteps in our relationship evaporate into thin air, however, we all know that is not how life works. Some of the battles we fought for and against each other taught us that we were worth fighting for. They made us stronger and they revealed to us how much we had to lose.

If you asked both Brandon and I, independently, what the best day of our life has been we would honestly agree it was our wedding day. Surrounded by all the people that witnessed our first date, watched our love grow and bloom for seven years, while even sharing our struggles, we felt more joy than we could have imagined the day we were wed. Those of you that are mothers are probably shaking your heads thinking that the birth of our three children should be ranked first. I will concede that the days my children entered this world were spectacular life-changing moments. My heart felt physically *larger* than it did the day before, like the Grinch in the ever-popular Christmas special. But the first time my heart grew *stronger* than it ever had was when I held my husband's hand and told the rest of the world that we would triumph together. It was truly the most fabulous day of my life.

We have been married ten years now. He is still that strong, sensitive soul that I can depend on when obstacles present themselves. I am still the girl who knows what she wants and goes after it. I am mouthy, where he is quiet. I am introspective and prefer quiet settings, where he is more spontaneous and thrives when the radio is cranked to maximum volume. A few of our traits have changed while we grow older together, some of which have created anxiety or uncomfortable moments from time to time. I have become a dreamer, where he is a doer. I crave intellectual conversations where they often make Brandon squirm. He enjoys creating, renovating, and enhancing things and rarely sits down to enjoy his accomplishments. I rather enjoy the sitting down part. Where he has become more driven, I have become more complacent. Meeting in the middle is an art form that still eludes us from time to time. Common interests that have developed over time have helped us see past the differences, however. Renovating our home, enjoying summer concerts together, taking pleasure in our yearly beach vacations, all remind us of what we do have in common. Even the occasional afternoon spent rock-wall climbing, kayaking or participating in other thrill-seeking adventures are dates we enjoy *sans* our children. The truth is that we have a lot of history for only being in our early thirties. With that comes a sense of comfort in each other, but also the challenge to keep things new and interesting.

Brandon and I are those high school sweethearts that can both tug on your heartstrings and make you want to throw up, in one fell swoop. In these seventeen years, we are no longer fearless and self-absorbed. We cannot be. We have three little people depending on us. That alone is awe-inspiring and completely overwhelming. I am no longer just a girl and he is no longer just a boy. We blinked, just a little too long, and we have become a man and a woman doing this crazy thing called Life together.

chapter eighteen

set my circus down

Years ago, before we had children, Brandon and I would wake up on a Saturday morning, realize we had nowhere to go and nowhere to be, and we would spontaneously jump in the car and go for a drive. I know, it sounds kind of like Driving Miss Daisy-ish, or a past time that is reserved for the over-sixty crowd maybe. But we loved it. We loved the open road, the wind in our hair, and the endless possibilities of adventure. It was also the way we shared our dreams with each other. At that time we were living on the Northwest side of Atlanta where you do not have to drive far to find money. Big money. And the both of us being twenty-three years old, one an engineer and the other a chiropractic student, we would inevitably find ourselves driving through some pretty doctor-esque neighborhoods, dreaming about *our* future money. Homes with a minimum of five bedrooms, granite covered counters, imported Italian flooring and foyers the size of our then current home. We could not dream large enough. We loved the gated communities. We would gaze in from the outside of the gate, admiring the beautifully manicured sidewalks, superbly clean and decorator-decorated front porches. There were porch swings and topiaries gracing the front porches, standing like sentries to the castle within. These homes were not built with brick, it is more appropriate to say that they were adorned with brick and stone flown in from some distant land. And of course the vehicle so proudly displayed on the cobblestone driveway, with grass growing up the middle like a private runway, was as spectacular a sight as the house itself. The car was always black, sleek, with a rounded contour like a woman gracefully lying on her side. Tan leather within, not a speck of dust on the dashboard, and still smelling like a new car. *Always* smelling like a new car. The lawns in these neighborhoods were impeccably maintained, like Monet himself sat down with the homeowner and designed it personally. There were flowering potted annuals in huge, ceramic pots that probably cost more than our car payment that month. Ferns framing the front door, the side door, the garage door, the backdoor. No entrance to the fortress was without adornment. There were fences that served no containment purposes, but rather served as visual delineation of yet another gorgeous piece of earth that the owners felt needed visual attention and respect.

Thinking back on this I actually remember enjoying this past time with Brandon even back in high school when we were newly dating. Now if you knew Brandon back then you might have a hard time envisioning this. You have to understand that Brandon had a reputation to keep up with as Football Player, Football T-shirt Wearer, I Forgot to Comb My Hair Today Guy, and Watch How I Can Eat Eight Sandwiches Today Stud. But it turns out that Brandon had a depth to him that most people were unaware of. He was more than just a football, basketball, softball playing stud. He slowly revealed talents, dreams and a pure enjoyment for architecture. He loves clean lines, sturdy structure, and perfection in form and function. For several years while Brandon was a teenager, his father was building the Hellenbrand family's dream house. From my understanding, Brandon spent many Saturdays helping his father install drywall, trim, cabinets, and fixtures in order to make this new home ready to move into. He was rewarded with actually getting to live in this house for a couple of years prior to moving out for college. While still in high school he signed up for a drafting class that allowed him to design his own dream house. My future husband's neurology was wired such that even back then he was far more left-brained than right-brained. Though he was never placed into advanced math courses like calculus while in high school, he had a terrific talent to actually understand and apply the math principles of which I was only able to memorize and regurgitate, but never actually comprehend. Geometry and the study of spatial relationships, along with the physics principles that blurred my thought processes simply flowed through his synaptic clefts to forever reside there for future need. And the most beautiful part of these talents of his were that they created a road into which he could travel down into the right side of his brain and *dream* a little with me.

Dreaming is not something that comes natural to Brandon. Dreaming does not follow any laws of physics, or even logic. There is no outline to follow, no rulebook, step-by-step manual or necessary expectations. Your dreams can be way out there, or they can be within reach. It does not matter. They can have a logical progression of what comes next, or they can throw logic out the window and be akin to trying to catch a shooting star instead. *This is why I love to dream.* And for the same reasons, this is why

Brandon can struggle with it. Those Saturday morning drives allowed us to meet in this beautiful middle space like a secret layer of the stratosphere that no one else knew about. Just the two of us could fly in there, gently nod our heads at each other, and start gazing out into the unknown landscape below us. Our enjoyment together, doing what I now refer to as "dream shopping" therefore had an early start. The allure of beautiful homes was a common place for us to meet, study, and dream simultaneously.

It is equally fascinating to me how much one's dreams can change as the years go by. Fast forward twelve years, insert into the equation three children, two dogs, a Stay-at-Home-Mom status, and temperate Georgia living, and suddenly the dream of a gated community with a bunch of stuff on my picturesque front porch does not seem as appealing to me. First off, I now drive a *mini-van*. I swore it would not happen, but then the third kid came along and it seemed better than buying a Suburban that I would need to use a stepstool to launch myself into. (Remember, I am "small-framed" we will call it.) The doctor degree no longer facilitates extreme purchases, but rather dictates frugality so we can pay the student loan for said doctor degree. There was no way for me to foresee my desire to spend my days talking kid-speak, planning play dates, or having Hasbro-game-a-thon afternoons on rainy days, and the sad truth is that school loans need to be paid even if the degree isn't being utilized. In fact I would have argued against the mere possibility of my life being what it actually is today and yet I find myself in a self-described happy place. Every one of those things I do as a stay-at-home-mom is what I choose whole-heartedly to do for as long as I am blessed to do them.

Here I sit however, ready to openly admit (while simultaneously hanging my head in shame) that I am ready for *additional blessings*. Sounds kind of demanding of God and the universe, *I know*. But the truth is that we are ready for a new adventure. And the absolutely unbelievable part of that statement is that *we*, collectively, are ready. In the past it has always been one of us that was ready for a nine-hundred-mile move south, ready for a dog, ready for another dog, a new house, a child (okay, two are fine) – and in this chronological order, please Mr. Universe. So now we find ourselves in unknown territory where we are sharing new dreams. That will make things infinity easier, I think. These dreams may be coming from far left field, granted. But they are ours and we own them.

So here it is: we want a farm. We want to live in an old farmhouse with architecturally charming features, where we can look out our windows and see a horse or two grazing on our pasture. I love those words. *Our pasture.* Not someone else's pasture across the street or down the road on my commute to drop the kids off at school. Our pasture. A pasture where we can put a couple of goats or horses that will romp and play with our two mutts. Our children will run and explore the land in the way that only children can. There will be new bugs to collect, new trees to climb, and a bell to ring when they have disappeared for too long and need to check in. Oh, and I want a sign on our pasture fence down by the road that reads, "Please drive safely, children and animals at play." I envision a room full of windows where I can read, knit, scrapbook, or write while overlooking all of these wonders of nature. I am certain that I would witness grace on this farm. My how dreams change, huh?

So when I think about those homes I used to envy and dream of owning, those homes that look more like fortresses keeping people out rather than inviting people in, I pick up on other previously unseen features of those neighborhoods. There are few, if any, children running joyfully through those pristine lawns. No dogs romping around behind the fences, greeting the neighbors. There is no one actually sitting on that sparkling white porch swing, or even sitting inside their parlor or foyer gazing onto the beauty that is their yard and home. And so it turns out that this is not actually what I dream of anymore. I have found myself, again, in unfamiliar dream territory.

There is a country song sung by Tim McGraw that I have always loved. The lyrics are about the searching, the dreaming, and ultimately the place you want to call home. He makes reference to the "circus" that is his family and that description really jives with me. What parent cannot at one time or another describe their family as a circus? Okay, there are admittedly a few of these families out there. I have witnessed these Stepford Wife-type families and want nothing to do with them. I know their children never speak out of turn, never burp at the dinner table, and certainly never do "the underwear dance" while parading through the living room. I, however, would miss some of that adventure, excitement and joy. As parents we attempt to be the ringleaders, bringing order and joy, success and triumphs while simultaneously striving for laughter, and new talents discovered. It is the joy and the laughter that those little munchkins will reminisce about with their own children one day. The singular element of this circus life that I gave too little consideration was just how often we would find ourselves packed up and on a road to a new city or town, in search of yet another new and wonderful adventure. We are a *traveling* circus it turns out.

So this past Saturday, in the fall of 2009, when Brandon and I were assessing the possibilities for a free and unscheduled day, we decided to go *dream shopping* again. We both feel ready for an adventure. We want to feel the excitement that our own children have at nightfall, squinting into the darkness trying to find a firefly to catch. We are hoping for something magical, something we can wrap our arms around and take home with us. So we packed a lunch for the kids and informed them we were going on an adventure. They gave us questioning looks and inquisitive pleadings of, "but *where* are we going?" It is funny how when strapped into their car seats they are only interested in the destination. Of course, we do not have a destination and we refrain from sharing that little bit of information. A few books and toys in the name of distraction and off we go to dream shop.

Enter the farmette. Set on seven acres, this new and improved kind of kingdom we find has two pastures, an acre-size pond, and a genuinely charming home with a winding driveway, maple trees acting like sentries. This does not resemble a fortress, or even a freestanding castle, there are just too many trees and open space for that designation. There is the main home built grandly into an A-frame with an astonishing amount of windows and exposed beams. There are outbuildings that serve as visual focal points on an otherwise unspoiled landscape of green grass, mature trees, and a pond with hungry bass creating swirls on a smooth-as-glass surface. I am ferociously brought back to reality by the children screaming in octaves that actually make my ears bleed that "We are *starving* back here!" and "Can't we just *go somewhere???*" Reality check. It is time to wipe the drool off my chin, pat my husband gently on the knee because he is also in la-la-land, and graciously pop a DVD into the movie player. Yep, this mini-van thing is awesome.

So will we set this circus of ours down on this little farm? Or any farm, for that matter? I really do not know. There are many things to think about, things we have never really had to consider before. What is a bush hog and do we rent one or buy one? How do you paint a kitchen white that has dark wood trim throughout? Would we kill ourselves (or each other) trying to share a single-sink master bathroom until we can afford to renovate it? And who in God's name decided to put green carpet throughout this dream house of ours? I would like to have words with that person. Will we be lonely on the outskirts of town and start dreaming about gated communities again? There may not be any answers to these questions, of course. There may not be a rhyme or reason to what lies ahead for us. That realization can be a little unsettling and yet looked at another way can be the adventure we are seeking. Where will we set our circus down? What comes next for us? On this journey that has already been fifteen years in the making, it is impossible to know where we will end up. I remind myself that as long as my people are still my people, that as long as our family unit is still a unit, all will be well. Slow down and breathe, Kristi. This too is part of the ride.

chapter nineteen

remember Mama

"Remember Mama," comes out of Blake's mouth at least twenty times a day. Remember Mama, that I can wear my sandals today because I do not have school. Remember Mama, it is my turn (not my brothers) to pick which seat I want in the car. Remember Mama, that not every school bus is magic, like The Magic School Bus. Oh, God I want to. I want to remember *all of this*, Blake. I guess that is one reason why I began this project to begin with. No matter how much I want my life to slow down, or how much I want it to speed up, I most definitely want to remember this life. I want to remember the way these crazy kids yell, "MAMA, I'M DONE!" loud enough for the neighbors to come running, when they need their little hinies wiped. It is an unpleasant job, but their alert system puts a smile on my face every time.

The fact of the matter is that they will not need me so much later on. I suspect I will miss that very much. Not the hiney wiping, per se, but many other things. I will miss reading stories to them at night. I will miss helping them assemble their Lego sets. Gone will be the days when they will narrate their favorite cartoons to me, or when they will announce the latest bit of trivia they have just learned about egg-eating snakes. Granted, there will be other things I will do for them like driving them to sleepovers, baseball practice, or dropping them off at the movie theater to meet their friends. I will probably have to jumpstart their car for them, or maybe pick them up from a party they do not have a safe ride home from. What I will miss the most though are the hugs and cuddles I receive on a daily basis. My boys have been bestowed with a gentle nature and though I realize the spontaneous arm rubs I get from Blake when we are lying together on the couch will be no longer, I hope that the tilt of his head accompanied by his sweet "doe eye" look of love will present itself from time to time. Or maybe just a smile from across the room. I will settle for that. Of course it will be a capital offense should I request or initiate a public display of affection, but behind closed doors I like to think these "Mama's boys" will always be Mama's boys.

Now, Brooklynn on the other hand, I need to be more careful with. She is more fragile, and has a gentler nature than I myself do and I suspect she will be more easily hurt if the wrong words come out of my mouth. She is my lesson in tenderness and unending forgiveness, as she gives them both so easily. I must tread carefully with her. I have fond memories of attending 4H classes with my mother, learning how to knit, sew, crochet, and arrange flowers in an aesthetically pleasing manner. I remember planting my first garden of green beans with my mother and I will never forget my first sleepover that she arranged for me after we moved to a new town. She let me invite an old friend Missy, from our previous hometown, and a new friend Kate, from our new town. I fell into bed that night feeling that life was just about perfect. Those are all things I would like to do for my own little girl one day. And much, much more. I want to hug her tight when her friends are mean to her, and listen when she needs to vent. I want to hand over the keys to the car and tell her to be safe and have fun. I want to let her know I trust her, and to praise her on her hard work. I want her to know that I love her unconditionally. Ultimately I want her to be a better person than I am. Inevitably, we will drift apart, as most mothers and daughters do, but I want to be there when she is ready to find her way back. The two of us are surrounded by boy toys, boy lingo, and boy macho and I hope we can be each other's anchor to girlhood. Everything from simple luxuries of getting our nails done together while chit-chatting over the men in her life, to enjoying a hot cup of coffee while she expresses the perils of motherhood with me. Cue me patiently listening and nodding and loving her unconditionally.

But enough of what I hope for the future, because I am brutally aware that none of those Norman Rockwell moments will occur without a tremendous amount of work and reflection on the immediate needs of my family. Time has proven repeatedly that those days *will come soon enough.* My children will grow up and lead lives of their own. The journey is what is truly sweet. So I will plow the ground, sow the seeds, and water the tender stalks. Through droughts and rainstorms, through sunny and cruddy, I will be there. "Remember Mommy," says Blake. Yes, baby, I am going to. I promise.

epilogue

We made that move I spoke about, to the country. Well, seven acres that happen to fall just inside the city limits but with the charm of country living. We have a barn, a pasture, a pond and endless possibilities for daily adventures. This is the life of my dreams that I carefully never coveted too much for fear of it not coming true. If I lived a former life, I rode horses over prairies, hung laundry out to dry, and took pride in feeding my family off the land. Nowadays I watch someone else's horses out on my pasture, carefully collect my own free-ranging eggs each evening, tend my small yet bountiful garden out back, and watch the sun go down on a beautiful Georgia landscape.

I am sitting in my comfy chair on my screened porch soaking up this beautiful spring morning in 2011. My coffee is freshly brewed and smelling wonderful, being the warm exception to the otherwise chilly morning. Our new rescue dog, Justice has his ears perked to the endless songs of birds greeting the new day, his nose lifted in appraisal when the rare breeze blows through. Copper is out running the perimeter of the yard, chasing squirrels and birds and anything else that has the audacity to visit his play space. My seven-year-old boys are at school enjoying their last few weeks of first grade before summer vacation washes over us like the first wave that greets you at the beach. There will be screams of delight, we all adore the summer season and the closeness it brings to our family. Gone will be the days when getting dressed and brushing our teeth are prerequisites for breakfast. No more grumpy cereal choices each morning, in favor of eggs and pancakes, French toast or maybe even peanut butter and jelly if the mood arises. There will be a calmness and sense of wonder each morning as the day begins slowly with a multitude of unknown activities and fun awaiting us. The children will revel in the thirty minutes of allowed cartoon time before beginning our day together, or may sleep through it if they so wish.

Until summer arrives however, my girl and I sit and enjoy this quiet morning. Brooklynn is upstairs playing with her dollhouse in a dreamy fairyland where ponies can sit down with princesses for an ice-cream breakfast. She loves this time to herself, without her brothers exclaiming that ponies do not drive cars and princesses are not real. There are no monster trucks attempting to swap paint with the princess carriage and the Taylor Swift CD playing in the background is without a moans-and-groans accompaniment. This is what we call "girl heaven" in our house.

Each day in our new home finds me slowing down and relaxing more than I did at our last place. Not because it is quieter here. In fact, it greatly surprised us when we discovered it is *twice as loud* here as it was in our suburbia neighborhood. Gone are the sounds of neighbors or tractor-trailers passing by. Those sounds have been replaced with birds chirping and chickens clucking over their morning breakfast. Horses whinny when we walk by, and deer greet us almost daily, meandering across the driveway looking at us as though *we* are the trespassers. My dogs raucously beg to differ, having a form of turf war with them. I find myself eavesdropping on the busy workings of a woodpecker, the meow of a lonely kitty wanting to join me on the porch, the loud clucking of hens arguing over a prime nesting spot, and the laughter of my children discovering yet another form of wildlife they never knew shared this heavenly world with us. Of course we are also privy to wildlife that we would prefer to not have run-ins with: wolf spiders as large as the palm of my hand, circling hawks hunting for chickens, snakes taking up residence in the barn, beavers moving into the pond, tomato horn worms in the garden, and an unbelievable number of frogs croaking and singing so loudly that they literally chase us off the porch each night.

Being surrounded by all of this newness, we were initially (and ridiculously, I might add) surprised to find that our day-to-day happenings were much the same here, however. We still have teeth to brush, meals to prepare, a home to clean, and most importantly, children to raise. It is our downtime that seems to have morphed into something that is from another century. Or as author, Barbara Kingsolver and many others suggest, quite possibly a lifestyle we will all need to return to in the very near future. We watch less TV (without the mandatory unplugging ceremony other families have instituted). We invite our friends over more now, feeling they should also enjoy the respite a couple of hours here can deliver. And quite frankly, each new day seems to bring an unexpected visitor to our home, be it a girlfriend who was just driving by, or a lone goose who while flying over our pond found it to be the perfect rest stop.

Being more aware of your home, your land, and the wildlife you share it with also inherently makes you more aware of the people sharing your space. I see a sense of purpose and pride in Brandon's eyes when he completes a job that others would consider a chore. A new roof on the barn is a great accomplishment and worth every drop of sweat it demanded. When he fixes the crack in the well pipe and then discovers three other cracks needing repair, he derives satisfaction in knowing the work he does will enable us to water our lawn, our horses, and the garden, without a concern over county water usage restrictions. My Blake has discovered a love for our kitten that he has never shown for another animal ever in his life. He holds her, he talks to her and I have found it immensely endearing to watch him grow in this way. In addition, his lack of enthusiasm for chicken chores or romps with the dogs can easily be forgiven when I witness his genuine fascination in the garden. His lone sunflower is a foot taller than any of mine, proving he has quite the green thumb.

Tristan, on the other hand, truly enjoys cleaning out the chicken coop. He is more than willing to collect eggs for me and commonly will engage the filly in a nose rub. I have witnessed him shoveling river rock with his father and building carp traps in the garage. He has become a fisherman, able to pluck a dragonfly from mid-air and turning it into live bait that a large mouth bass cannot resist. My little angel Brooklynn is a nurturer and no place like a farm can deliver the opportunities to expound on that skill. Each baby chick has a name. Each duckling receives a love tap. Little Miss Blacky, our rescue kitty, is her baby for all intents and purposes. She feeds her, holds her, loves her and talks to her like a friend. The cat eats it up. Being that I am allergic to cats and am a self-professed *dog person*, I am continually amazed at our good fortune for having found such a sweet kitten to bless our home.

We have set our circus down, at least for a time, somewhere that will define our family life in ways we were unaware of when we made the purchase of this property. There will still be little league games for the boys and gymnastics classes for Brooke. My children still enjoy couch jumping, videogames, and ice-cream sandwiches as big as their heads. However, in the past seven months they have also spent afternoons beaver hunting with their father, hours engrossed by a mouse-sized spider that even a Google search left unidentified, and learning the difference in yolk color (and hence nutritional value) of a free-range organic egg versus that of the commercially grown Leghorn egg bought for cheap at Wal-Mart. This is more of that priceless stuff that I love so much.

The challenges of raising children are still present in our lives. My sweet little girl, now five years old, has the ability to morph into something from the swamp when she feels the need. Temper tantrums occur on a daily basis, but they are thankfully followed by an "I'm sorry Mommy" squeak when her nerves have settled. Tristan and Blake still have an incredible amount of boy energy and have become competitors to the nth degree. One is always trying to out-do, out-talk and out-smart the other, receiving a scowl or shove in return. It is still exhausting, it is still beyond my understanding, but it is what it is. All of my children still have very soft hearts and abound with generosity. They still wrap me in their arms and smother me with their love and affection. I am eating it up. Soon my little boys will be eight years old and new and different things will come to pass. I am filling up my gas tank with these beautiful moments to sustain me through the difficult ones.

No, life is not always beautiful. My favorite dog Tyson, my baby, is buried down by our pond. We lost him this spring to a stomach ailment that slowly wasted him away. His favorite swimming spot has become his final resting place and I am still coming to grips with the end of what feels like an era. His dog tag now rests next to Oakley's on the picture frame from 2003.

Oh, and did I mention that my friend Laura has been diagnosed with breast cancer? Living with the mantra "It is what it is" becomes more difficult when cancer meets you on the road and tries to run you over. She is doing it though. In fact, she is *more than* doing it. She is beating it. She is declaring life is beautiful *even still.*

Make no mistake, my temper still flares, tears still fall and I still have a tendency to throw into question everything I do as a mother. Introspection can be a powerful tool to assess and better oneself. It can also be a terrible weight to carry if practiced too often. So I try to quiet my mind, observe and simply *be.* I can report that in the years it has taken me to write this book, I have mellowed that Type A personality a bit, come to appreciate the unique and spontaneous adventures we have found ourselves on, and I have a greater respect for the blessings that my husband and children are to me. I am more patient and forgiving of both my family *and myself,* finding it profits all of us to do so.

Coming in from the chicken yard yesterday filthy and smelling of the baby chicks we had been handling, little Brooklynn said to me, "Mama, my nose is too tickly to wash my hands." She is fully aware that returning from the barn requires hand washing, of which she prefers to avoid at all costs. Her excuse however, puts a smile on my face, having never been in that particular "tickly" predicament myself. I shoot her a jovial look of astonishment and offer my own fingers to cure the itch, fully recognizing the clown-like behavior that has come to define my amiable and innocent little girl. My, how these little people of mine have changed and my, how quickly. It feels like yesterday when I was teaching them how to walk. Now we are teaching them to shoot bee-bee guns and walk in their first princess heels. This new place and home that I find myself in is *my happy place*. I continue to record our lives and take in the extraordinary beauty that is my family. I sincerely strive to be present in my life.

And so to conclude, I hope that this story was a gift to you. That in some small way it helped you recognize the exquisiteness of your own life, the beauty that you are inevitably surrounded by. My deepest hope is that you are stronger as a mother and as a woman for having read it. I know it has been a gift to me and mine. Now, if you will excuse me, Brooklynn wants to play a game of Snakes and Ladders over a warm cup of cocoa and I will not let this opportunity pass.

acknowledgments

In the three and a half years that it has taken me to write this book there have been countless people that inspired and shaped its creation. Some of these wonderful souls you have read about in the preceding pages, some you have *unfairly* not. So it is here that I give mention and appreciation for those who helped me (in both large and small ways) with such an amazingly fun chapter of my life.

For all of those who encouraged my love of reading, and taught me early on to challenge myself: Dad, it almost goes without mentioning(smile); Grandpa Worachek, your shining smile and pride in me pushed me forward, even from the grave. Uncle Jim Worachek, I do so love you and appreciate the many years you devoted to being such a role model to me.

To all of you whom I reference in this book, especially Laura Soper and the extended Furman family, Ed Bernhards, Mike Carreria and Nancy Salguiero, Jackie Ballweg, Larry Kopf, Angie Stevens, Claire Sinnot, Laura Bender, and the three people who helped bring my babies into this world safe and sound (Claudia, Debbie and Doc Angel), you all have shaped my life into what is it today. From the bottom of my heart, I appreciate each and every one of you.

A special thank you to the lovely gentleman who brought Oakley home to me on a blanket. You did not have to take the time and you did. May the world smile upon you and yours.

A warm thank you to Father Victor Galier, the women of Women's Faith Formation, and the entire St. Matthew's parish family, for so gently and lovingly showing me what Catholic living can be.

To a dear friend who was barely mentioned when she should have been *highlighted* within my pages, Melissa Kotch you have been "the steady" in a time when things have been anything but. Your brilliant theories to explain the trials of motherhood, your cool and collected demeanor when you transported my lovies to and from Pensacola hospital and saved me from myself…you are an amazing person and I feel truly blessed to know you. I cannot forget to mention the amazing work you did for me creating the cover of my book. You allowed me countless edits, patiently created a piece of my dream, and were always good for a girls' night out and a glass of red wine. Girl, I love you.

Sarah Korreck, thank you for asking *Ed* to prom.

My dear sister Chelle, who constantly reminds me of my strengths when I feel most weak and is a true reflection of the undying love every mother should have for their children, you are *such a good mom.*

A warm and heartfelt hug to the entire Hellenbrand family, many of whom I have carefully observed and studied these past years as they were raising their own children. I have learned a lot from all of you, most of all *your* mother and father. There is no greater loyalty from a father and no greater genuine love from a mother than I have had the privilege to witness as a member of your extended family. Richard and Mary Beth, you are both such an inspiration to me. Without the two of you in our lives, many joys may not ever have come to pass. Thank you from the bottom of my heart.

Dad, you were one of my first reviewers of this book and your words of advice helped me find my audience and nail down my ultimate goal. Thank you for that. For my entire life you have stood by my side as witness to my strengths and weaknesses, achievements and failures. More importantly you have found the ability to love me through them all. You are my honest-to-goodness hero.

Mom, thank you for reading this. Thank you for allowing me creative expression, honesty in my writing and the ultimate healing that has come from sharing our lives. Our relationship has always been complicated, but I am coming to realize that the people that make us the most uncomfortable at times are the very people we are supposed to learn something from. Your story *is* one of grief, abuse, secrets, illness, loneliness and great loss. It is a testament to you and Dad that mine is not. If you did not hear it clearly enough in the written words within this book, my heart still aches for you and I only want happiness for you. Go and seek it.

Last, but never least, my darling Brandon, thank you. For believing in me, for understanding me, for choosing *me* to spend your life with. You have made my heart's dreams a reality. As Brooklynn would put it, I love you to Pluto and back.

CPSIA information can be obtained at www.ICGtesting.com
Printed in the USA
244673LV00001B/1/P